BLACK EMERALD

The IV Dynasty Vol.II

BLACK EMERALD

The IV Dynasty Vol.II

By

Henry Vereen IV

ISBN: 0-75960-776-1

This book is printed on acid free paper.

1stBooks - rev. 2/14/01

TABLE OF CONTENTS

Part 1

Henry Vereen IV

Blaq Ice

The feel of money, it's the most sensual feeling to my fingertips. The drive for it, its like destiny untold, trampling anything in my path, anything opposing that goal. Can you feel me, the soul it creates, I hate to say is faithful to sin. True to the path it lays, damn I had to follow it. Now destined to run this dynasty, once rolled five strong, but four generals dropped, leaving me to hold the bloody chips.

Its been three years since Shamon's death, my new soldiers a young squadron headed by Rush. The squadron: Korlane, Ducane, Mojo and Brandy. They kept the business tight throughout the northeast. Leroy down south, was surprise in how he handles his business. IN San Francisco, Berlin still ran his business foolishly, but his link to our now silent partner, Cruisian Ramone was vital to our success.

In Texas, Ron Plato, my Compadre kept most of the F.B.I. on the payroll. My grounds with BaiRute was still shaky, his crew was my national loot gatherers. Shamon would've been happy, Shays Point is still rolling strong, almost two million a year, envious businessmen now seek my advice. As I cruise in my Hummer, I smile to myself as I see Shays Point. Standing in front of the club parking lot was Brandy, her dark complexion hid the redness of her skin.

I slowly pulled up beside her, in her face I could see her frustration. I rolled my window down, her eyes then focus on me. "Black, I got to talk to you" Brandy spits out, her words clearly pronounced.

"Yea, I'll talk to you inside". I said to Brandy calmly. Brandy then turns and walks into the club. Brandy being alone was unusual because she was usually with Mojo. I took my time parking in the back. I stepped out of the car, I saw two Benz's and a Jaguar also parked in the back. These are the other crew member's cars. From this I knew something was wrong. So I quickly got to the back door of the club's office. Once inside I saw somber looks on everyone's face, but Mojo wasn't present.

"Where's Mojo?' I asked Rush,, my right-hand dog. Rush hesitated to answer, from that I got a feeling, that nigga was dead or either seriously hurt.

"Mojo got shot on Harlem Ave., he's in the hospital." Rush says his emotions in check, something that took him years to master. I glanced at the rest of the weary crew, before I asked another question. The crew sat with their heads down, all of them feeling guilty about the incident.

"Why was he by himself?" I asked Rush, Rush looked at me with cold eyes.

"He wasn't, I was with him. We were pumping Hakeam and Cortez for information. Things just went wrong." Rush says, the stare he had affixed on my eyes, was a pulsating burn. I broke the stare as I once again looked over the crew. Korlane was his usual relaxed self, as was Ducane, Brandy was shook up because Mojo was her partner in crime. I placed my cane next to my desk, before I sat down.

I took a deep breath, as silence befell the room, this was the first time either one of the crew has been through this. I relaxed, hoping, these young thirsty protégés would follow my lead. The atmosphere in the room, was stormy as everyone was drowning in the rain of being alarmed. The crew's so young, so wet that its laughable. The phone rang, disrupting the caressing silence. I picked up the phone on its second ring.

"Yo", I said, on the other end I could hear faint breathing. "Yo, this BaiRute, my team's in place." BaiRute retorts his northern accent drifts as he speaks. BaiRute's team was ready for their trip to San Francisco. This'll be his first trip to the west coast. I'm sending him, Donaven, and Tate. I'm sending them there so they can keep an eye on Berlin and Crusian. In my blood I could feel something was up with them. I didn't care too much for Berlin's sneaky ways, Crusian the same.

4

"Awright, pick your tickets up at the airport, call me when ya'll get there." I told BaiRute, then hung up the phone. The crew was now raising their heads. They all abruptly left, if something was to provoke them, any of them. I felt sorry for whom ever, I slowly pulled a Queen cigar, bit off the end, placed it in my mouth, then raised my lighter. As I puffed, the charismatic smoke rose in a scented cloud. The cigar burned steadily, as did my thoughts.

I wasn't trying to go to San Fran, too many memories of Mexico would surface. Don't get me wrong I love the women, the drank of hot fluids. San Fran just not my place of choice for right now. My thoughts are disturbed by a slight knock on the door. I looked up and saw this beautiful blend of Puerto Rican and Black. This female was nice, her eyes a dark brown. Her tone was a Siena Brown, I invited her into my office.

"What can I do you?" I asked the lady, her eyes were sparkling as she seamed to gather her thoughts.

"I heard you have a job opening for a waitress." The lady says, her accent smooth in tone. I sat for a moment, just checking out this lady's true credentials.

"So what's your name?" I asked this abstract blend of beauty. She smiled.

"Toi Sanchez." The lady says, her smile now a sly grin. I took a pull off my cigar, I knew she had the job. this would be the woman I was going to take up with.

"Mrs. Sanchez, I hope you enjoy working here at Shays Point. How soon can you start?" I said to Toi Sanchez, her smile became slight sigh of relief.

"Anytime." She says, her voice echoing her enthusiasm. I smiled at her once more.

"How's Friday sound, be here early, so we can issue you a uniform." I said to this beautiful lady. Toi Stood up as did I, and we shook hands. Toi then started towards the door, I watched her walk, how her hips moved like precise notes. I shook my head in rare excitement, as I then sat back down. My thoughts quickly returned to my situation and worries out west, in San Francisco. Throughout this time, things would get deep, relax and let me explain.

BaiRute's plane landed in San Francisco two days later. The afternoon heat was usual, for in California sun, was almost a constant. BaiRute, Donaven, and Tate collected their luggage before BaiRute called me. I told BaiRute that he had a room at the Grand Doscine in San Francisco. BaiRute was in the mind set to put Berlin out of the dynasty for good. I couldn't afford to have an inner conflict, the dynasty would suffer mad money lost.

BaiRute and Tate were now sitting in the hotels lobby waiting on Donaven to join them. Once all three of them were together they headed out to Berlin's place. Berlin's place was almost like a palace. The outside had white marble pillars, as they stood on a marble floor they gleamed in the Cali sun. BaiRute and his entourage finally arrives at Berlin's place. To greet them at the door was Berlin's right hand, Charlie Diggs.

BaiRute was silent as he Donaven and Tate were being escorted across Berlin's grassy front lawn. The walkway was laced on the side with white roses. Charlie Diggs opened the front door to Berlin's lavish spread. Inside, BaiRute marveled at the sights, women were all around, dressed in bikinis, some were topless. Donaven and Tate also shared BaiRute's view, which was extensive. Standing in a doorway close enough for BaiRute to see him, standing was Berlin.

"BaiRute, my nigga, what up?" Berlin says, in his voice concern was flowing in disguise. BaiRute took notice to Berlin's fake tone, then followed up Berlin's question.

"What up Baby, I'm saying this shit here is tight." BaiRute says, his comment basically meant for the ladies.

"Shit, I'm glad you like it. So I guess Black wants his money. That is why y'all are out here?" Berlin says, his eyes focused on BaiRute's eyes. Before BaiRute answered Berlin's questions, Berlin's wood grain cellular phone, started ringing. Berlin quickly answered the phone.

6

"Yea who this?" Berlin asked, his voice almost a whisper. On the other end a man was gathering his response.

"Yes, this is Crusian, I'm in Vegas at the Dune meet me there in three hours." Crusian says then hangs up. Back on Berlin's end Berlin showed BaiRute to his office, where they sat and talked. Donaven and Tate sat patiently, their attention was on the women approaching them from down the hallway. On the inside of Berlin's office BaiRute was just about pissed off.

"What! Man get the fuck out of here, where's the money?" BaiRute says trying not to loose his element. Berlin shook his head, as he then spoke, to an irritated BaiRute.

"I'm saying, I want to offer you a chance, to join me in getting Black out of the way" Berlin says his eyes gleaming from his scandalous thoughts. BaiRute's eyes then drop to the floor, his mind in deep thought. "BaiRute, he cut you out of the main money, he uses you as his lackey. Man, I wouldn't take that shit." Berlin says, as to add extra incentive on BaiRute's thoughts. "I tell you what, I'm a give you sometime to think this out." I got an appointment. Charlie will show you out."

Berlin says as he walks out of his office. BaiRute slowly walks out, collecting his two men. BaiRute, Donavan and Tate, then left the lavish house of Berlin's. BaiRute was quiet in their rent a car, as he evaluated betraying me. BaiRute let Berlin's words flow on his mind's vibe. Between the two of us, BaiRute weighed his options, Black or Berlin his thoughts shifted back and forth. BaiRute shook his head as this was the most thinking he's ever had to do.

Tate and Donaven was talking amongst themselves in the front seat, they both noticed BaiRute's quiet disposition.

"That nigga is about to flip on someone." Tate says to Donaven with his eyes focused on the road as he drove. Donaven glared at BaiRute in the rear view mirror. Then looked back out the window.

"I'm seeing that look in his eyes, wondrous and shit." Donaven says to an agreeing Tate.

"Word, word, he's on that mental note. I think that talk with Berlin got his head." Tate says, his voice escalating in excited tones. Donavan's eyes roll back to the rearview mirror, as he began once again to peer at BaiRute. This time BaiRute caught Donavan's peering eyes in a unconcerned frown. Donavan's eyes shift from the mirror to the window, where they remained, for the remainder of the drive back to their hotel. Back down in Vegas, Crusian was plotting my demise awaiting Berlin's arrival.

"This is my operation, without me there isn't a so called dynasty." Crusian says to his lackey, Bruce, who sat with a cheesy grin on his face. Crusian laughed a little, as the blow he snorted earlier had him high in his mind. His laughter stopped as he saw Berlin walking through the door with Tee-Mason at this side. Berlin's eyes was set on Crusians entourage, he was scooping their faces, seeing their thoughts in their eyes.

Berlin knew he was alright, and could go on with the plan with Crusian. Crusian's plan was to play me close, get into my peoples' heads, and cause a coup. Berlin has on his side unknowingly BaiRute and his crew. Berlin and Crusian sat and talked about their collaborated scheme.

"There's a problem." Berlin says, his words as serious as his facial expression. Crusian's frown, which was steady on his face, became a cold stale expression.

"What problem?" Crusian says through his cold expressionless face. Berlin's eyes dropped to the table he was sitting at. Then he slowly spoke.

"Rush, that nigga's gonna be trouble." Berlin says, his eyes still situated on the table.

"Do you have BaiRute's cooperation? If so then we'll have him get rid of Rush and possibly Black." Crusian says then cracks a rare smile. Berlin's eyes raise up, to meet Crusian's eyes in a conjunction of cold stares. The two of them didn't trust the other because of past beefs. Crusian wanted sole control of the dynasty, which meant getting me to become an irrelevant fixture in it.

True to his lavish ways, from the <u>Dune</u> to the strip, Berlin was out to gamble a couple of grands away. Crusian headed back to the Bay area, to handle his business. Cane, P.C.P., Crystal Meth. His business was the dynasty's nervous system. I could see why Crusian wanted to control it all. If he wanted it he had to take it. By me, I don't think he could handle the task.

On the strip Tee-Mason and Berlin was talking about their upcoming plan.

"I'm saying do you think BaiRute really is going to flip on Black?" Tee-Mason asks Berlin in an inquisitive tone. Berlin shook his head, marveling at Tee-Mason's question.

"Man, when BaiRute thinks of the money he's lost, shit, Black will be dead already." Berlin says, his smile stimulated from scheming thoughts. Tee-Mason shakes his head at Berlin's half thought out answers.

"Man, you forgot about Rush, that nigga and his squad aren't going to lay down and let BaiRute take Black. "Tee-Mason says to a now laughing Berlin. Tee-Mason decided to go with the flow, rather than run parallel to the situation. Back in San Fran BaiRute was calling Carlos in Long Island.

"Yo, what up baby? What's the shit on the west coast?" Carlos asks BaiRute whom was somewhat quiet on the other end.

"Crazy shit son, I'm saying shit's gonna get deep in a minute though." BaiRute says his mild tone was a warning sign to Carlos.

"Word, on what son. Berlin Fronted on the money." Carlos says his voice curious in tone.

"Naa, no shit like that. These niggas are plotting on Black to get him out of the picture." BaiRute says to his listening cousin. "I mean shit's about to get thick." BaiRute says his voice echoes unsureness of the situation.

"Damn son, so what you going to do. Lay low or join the shit. Me personally, I didn't being cut out of the money like that." Carlos says, giving BaiRute the hint, to join in removing me. BaiRute catching the hint hung up the phone, then called me here in Westgate.

"Yo, Black my nigga what's up? I got your money." BaiRute says, his voice was wavery. I ignored it, as I thought it was just extensive jet lag.

"You have a hassle?" I asked due to my own curiosity. BaiRute hesitated for a moment. The rarity of this, subdued my optimism.

"Naa, no hassle, shit was smooth in the transition." BaiRute says quickly coming out of his hesitation. I relaxed, holding back on questioning him more. "We'll be back in a few days." BaiRute says, then hangs up the phone, before I could respond. I shook my head as I knew then something was wrong. Back here in Westgate, I was now joined in my office by Brandy. Brandy was unusually quiet, her brown eyes cleared, of the water that glazed her eyes earlier.

"I saw Reese last night, He was over at my place last night." Brandy says, her voice little for shame. I looked at Brandy and grinned.

"And what's your point?" I asked Brandy, I was teasing her of her situation. Brandy and Reese was an 'on and off' thing. Reese is a key pusher on Chancellor Ave., and an informant of mine for the police. I send him false information, so when the police press him for information, they have an ear full of bull... to decipher. Then, I noticed the look Brandy had on her face. "Man come on, not raw, my man did it raw." I said laughing in between words.

"What you want, boy or girl?" I asked Brandy mockingly. Brandy's eyes became a cold slit. I knew from that look that Brandy was disappointed in my response. So I decided to make up for it.

10

"Yo, I'll get rush to handle him for you, in the meanwhile keep your legs closed." I clearly say to Brandy, from my last comment, she smiles. Meanwhile across town, Rush and Korlane was keeping my local street value steady. They sat talking in Rush's Benz.

"Man, them niggas right, was holding heat and still didn't shoot back." Korlane says, as his diamonds flashed in the car's pale moon roof light.

"Who, nigga?" Rush says, as he's frustrated by Korlane's usual non-descriptive ways. Korlane laughs as he then specifies whom he was speaking of.

"Them niggas right there, looking like hoes you." Korlane says, then sighs. "Yo, man I'm saying BaiRute's got me thinking on some flip shit.' Korlane says now drawing Rush's most serious attention.

"I hear you, BaiRute has that shit written in his eyes. Sooner or later he's gonna flip on Black." Rush says, Korlane nods his head in agreement.

"I'm saying what's to gain, so much heat would come down on the operation. Korlane says shaking his head in amazement of such an immense situation.

"I don't know, but if shit happens like that, keep your heat close baby." Rush says, as he watches the street corna's occupants, they were slanging those stones like crazy, talking loud, and popping noise. Meanwhile back in San Francisco, Berlin and Tee-Mason was now back in Berlin's place talking once against with BaiRute.

"So what's the deal?" Berlin asks BaiRute, whom sat deep in thought. BaiRute brought his eyes up to meet Berlin's stare.

"I'm with you, so how's this plotted out?" BaiRute says to Berlin in his calmest tone. Berlin smiled as he stared at BaiRute coldly. Berlin picks up his cellular phone, he quickly then dialed Crusians phone number. The phone rang four times, while Berlin was on the phone, BaiRute was lighting up some herb he rolled not so long ago.

11

"Yea, Crusian, the deal is set. BaiRute is with us." Berlin says his tone extremely calm. On the other end Crusian smiled to himself then spoke. "I'll be there tomorrow, til then, Berlin keep BaiRute happy." Crusian says then hangs up. Berlin now surrounded by the scent of herbal vapors, slowly put the phone down. BaiRute with no smile had his eyes affixed on Berlin's ice cold face. The teams circle, plotting my demise is now complete. BaiRute wasn't alone, as Donaven and Tate was also present, but in another part of the house.

Meanwhile here in Westgate Dugusne was on a solo mission, on his way to Naville to pick up 6 kilos of cocaine. Dugusne, didn't know this was a setup waiting to happen, with Cortez waiting on him at the meeting place. Rain was just falling, sprinkling the ground in various places. In the passenger seat next to Ducane was sitting his Smith and Wessen, looked for action. Once at the meeting place, the rain steadily picked up.

Cortez smiles at Ducane, as he watches Ducane exit his car. Ducane was lightly stunned to see Cortez by himself, this sight caused Ducane to tightly clutch his heat closer. In two more steps Ducane would be face to face with Cortez.

"Where's the merchandise?" Ducane asks, not knowing that what was about to happen would spark a war, within the dynasty. Cortez smiled, as he turned and waived to the occupants of his car. Ducane's facial expression was worth a million dollars, as he saw Kavasia exit the car Kavasia was one of Ron Platos right hand men, a trusted runner of the dynasty. Ducane knew from this a coup was about to occur on him.

"Here's your merchandise." Cortez says, as he now has his heat drawn. Being slow on the trigga, caused Cortez death as in a flash Ducane's Smith and Wesson was blazing. Ducane fires, till his gun was gutless. Kavasia was unimpressed as he raised his Beretta, in a quick orange colored flash, Ducane dropped to the wet ground. Blood was flowing from his torso in streams.

Kavasia, not once giving a second glance, turns and walks back to Cortez's black Lexus.

The Lexus driver Hakeam, slowly pulls away from the bloody scene. Till this day, I still don't get why they killed Ducane. That in itself was senseless. Why the waste of shells from heated barrels. The next day, the news of Ducane's death traveled fast. Mojo just got back from the hospital, the team was now militant in sight. I tried to ignore it, but hat was the same mistake Shamon made three years ago.

"First off, we're out-numbered. They'll be coming from every direction." I said to Rush, his ears grabbing every one of my words." From the west, Berlin is the biggest threat, down south Ron Plato. "I added, just to let Rush know the situation.

"What about Leroy in Carolina where's he stand?" Rush asks, his mind raving.

"He's with us, with his resources, we can hang with Berlin and Ron Plato." I said to Rush in a re-assuring way. As we sat in Shamon's office in Shay's Point. We carved out a strong plan to counter act whatever Ron Plato or Berlin come up with. I didn't let Crusian Ramone slip my mind, I kept him close in my thoughts. Things were about to get heavy, blood would flow at the end of these events. That much I suspect.

At this point, BaiRute was on his way back to the Island to gather his troops. Berlin and Ron Plato was already set, but one thing stopped them from making that crucial first move. They didn't know how to come at me. They didn't know my set up here in Westgate or the way my drugs or guns flowed. They didn't know the depth of my crews temperment. As far as they could tell, I was impervious to having an insider do me in.

[Two days later, Long Island]

"Damn, you know it's own, Black's gonna move soon son". Ramone says to BaiRute, whom was sipping on some Dry Gin.

"Man, it's going to be live as hell. But damn, what's that girl's name that hangs with Black's crew." BaiRute says, as he pours some more gin into his cup. BaiRute's comment to Ramone set his mind on fire, as Brandy's name finally came to light.

"Yea, Brandy, that's a fine jewel, son." Ramone says to a now smiling BaiRute. BaiRute took a sip of his Gin, before he responded.

"Word, Brandy, I'd bang the Hell out of that Jewel" BaiRute says shaking his head at the thought. A knock on Donavan's door disturbed the conversation, Donaven, whom was sitting next to Ramone, got up to answer it. Once the door was open, Carlos, Kingsmon, and Kremone was standing there, their cold expressions ever present on their faces. Donaven stepped back and let them walk in. Everyone except Tate was now at Donavan's place.

On the other side of town, blunt smoke was rising at a slow steam. This meeting between Tate and Rush was going to set the pace of the dynasty's war.

"To play both sides is going to cost my pocket's a few pounds. Their going to be thin." Tate says, with a wise smirk laugh on his harsh grill. Rush's eyes scan Tate's facial expression then smiles.

"Twenty grand should keep your pockets healthy. Every week at midweek at the mid hour, you report, ya feel me". Rush says as he hands Tate a sealed white envelope. Tate's sarcastic smirk became a cold frown. Rush watches Tate slowly walk away, a cool breeze was smoothly passing by Rush's arms and back. Rush then turns and starts toward his car. Rush pulls out of his left pocket a cellular phone and hits the speed dial button.

The phone on the other end rang three times before it was picked up.

"Yea, this Mojo, who this?" Mojo says his voice, secretely in pitch.

"This is Rush baby boy, yo the shits on, I want you and Korlane to stick close to Black. Tell Brandy I need to talk to her. Tell'er to meet me at my place. I'll check y'all out later." Rush says and then hangs up. Back over here at Shay's Point, I was talking to Korlane, whom was his usual distant self.

"I'm saying Black, this shit is going to be live, all the gun play and shit." Korlane says in a mocking manner. Even though he was being sarcastic, I shook my head in bewilderment of the trueness of the comment. "I'm saying, for real though, I know were going to come out on top." Korlane says, his voice now serious content.

"Kavasia, the right-hand of Ron Plato is running with Berlin and BaiRute, I got Rush handling some minor details to stay with them." I said to Korlane, my eyes roamed across Korlane's expressionless face. There was a slight knock on the office door. The atmosphere in the room started to thin out. Korlane went to the door and let himself out, as he left, Toi Sanchez entered. She was beaming her thick thighs filling out the shorts of her uniform.

"Yea, what's up lady?" I asked, I flashed a smile at her once I saw her face flush. In my thoughts, fantasies of her, wouldn't come close to the real physical beauty this lady possessed.

"I just wanted to know, if you think my uniform is appropriate?" Toi says, her voice as sweet as chocolate melting. I admired the below the waistline view, before I answered.

"I think the customers will be awright." I say to Toi then smiled, my nature flexing. Toi blushed, recognizing she was exposing a lot of thigh. Toi walked slowly out the door right when she exited the phone rang. "Yea." I said trying to focus, but Toi was slowly easing her way as my main thought process.

"Yea, Black, this Rush things are being set, Brandy though" Rush says then pauses.

"What about Brandy?" I asked Rush, during his brief hesitation. "I want to get her to fuck BaiRute for information. I mean put the nigga to sleep." Rush says, that answered my question.

"Yea, let me drop this 'kno' on you. Approach Brandy through Mojo, that seems to be a nigga that can tell her anything." I told Rush calmly. Rush on the other end was silent for a moment, then spoke.

"Yea, I'll catch up with him at the club. I'm out." Rush says then hangs up. I reared back in my leather chair. I decided to re-light my cigar. Simmering in thought, my mind now drifts. In a sentence could I describe my life, reminisce on Shamon and the rest of the crew. I shake my head, yes while smiling to myself. I could to it in one word. Hella-Trife.

Backsliding, ohhh backsliding. Makes me wonder what was the point of getting saved. Being blessed by the man up top, and cursed upon the ground I walk. I know my mom's is shaking her head at me, her spirit amused at my ways of being. Yea, I know I'm not perfect, but there is people worse than me on the sinners' list.

Back on the Island, BaiRute and his pistol gripping soldiers, were loading up into a two car caravan. Headed in Westgate's direction.

"Yo, we moving like hell on steel, grip ya shits tight we about to make history, Nigga!" BaiRute yells at Ramone, whom has a wild and willing grin on his face. Carlos, Donaven, and Tate was in that van also. Kingsmon and Kremone in the van that BaiRute was driving. Their favorite choice in weapons, streetsweepers, and magnums. They were set to make the seven hour trip, on a countdown to the start of a dynasty's civil war.

As the storm clouds gathered here in Westgate, Rush and Mojo was talking about Brandy. Unknowing of BaiRute coming here, his plan with Brandy, was irrelevant to the situation.

"Yea, -" Rush is interrupted by his cellular phone ringing. "Yo, who dis?" Rush says, his tone irritated by being interrupted in his conversation.

16

"Yea baby what's up, I'm on my way, I'm brining some company we'll be there in several minutes." The voice on the other end says then hangs up. Rush hung his phone up. Rush quickly placed the voice. Knowing it was Tate in his bones.

"Mojo, get Black on the phone. I'ma go to Shay's Point. Korlane and Brandy should be there." Rush says as he then bolts towards his car. Back to the caravan of BaiRute, BaiRute and his people was loading and cocking their weapons. Rain started to trickle as to BaiRute's right, a road sign read Westgate four miles.

BaiRute's mission, had him thinking about his past on the Island. Those same crossed feelings was starting to resurface in his thoughts. BaiRute's foot pressed harder on the gas, speeding up the confrontation. Down south in Texas, Ron Plato was at the airport, he was going to Samsonville. Samsonville was going to be the stronghold for the coup. Ron was engrossed in a conversation with Berlin on the cell phone.

"The shits started, I sent BaiRute as a distraction to give the situation a boost." Berlin says as he lets cigar smoke drift out of his mouth and nose.

"You make sure business is handled. This won't be no good if we loose street value. Keep Crusian close ya here, my boy." Ron Plato says then hangs up. On the other end Berlin took a puff of his cigar. Then a slight knock flowed across the rooms door. Berlin yelled for the person to enter. Charlie Diggs and Tee-Mason stepped over the door threshold first. Following them was Breana.

Breana was one of Candy's girls, whom of course, worked for me. Berlin met Breana in Westgate on his last trip there. Berlin waived off Tee-Mason and Charlie Diggs. They slowly left, Tee-Mason, the last out the door, left the door cracked slightly so he could keep an eye on the situation. Breana was on a suicide mission. Her task was to kill or mortally wound Berlin. Breana knew she wouldn't make it out alive.

"My nigga, you have enough security. It wouldn't be surprising if you had cameras in here." Breana says, her voice bitter sweet in tone. Her eyes roamed the room, searching for exposed weapons. Berlin just stood staring at Breana, smiling his thoughts dirty and exotic. Back in Westgate, things were about to get heated. The first confrontation of the coup.

BaiRute and his entourage was now on their way to Shay's Point. Rush and his people, were out to cut BaiRute and them off. This meeting would set it all off.

"Mojo ya'll got Shay's Point secured?" Rush yells into his cellular phone, the background behind Rush, clips being loaded and guns being cocked could be heard.

"Yea, everything here is just right baby." Mojo says his words carried an undoubtable tone of confidence. Rush hung up then and focused on his task. Soon, in sight, BaiRute's caravan was visible. Meanwhile back at Shay's Point, I was watching Mojo pace the floor in anticipation, I could feel his heart racing. Everything was quiet but in my third eye, I could see, and hear the fierce exchange of guns being fired.

Rush and BaiRute, the match of the century. It was brewing. I heard a car pull up to the back, with my nine ready, I sat fast, my mind was going militant, or as my boy Shamon would put it, mentally spasmodic.

Meanwhile in San Fran, Breana and Berlin was heavily into their sexual occasion. As Breana rode Berlin he laid still with his eyes closed.

Breana leaned slightly close to Berlin's face, and suddenly as she lifted her tongue, a silver metallic blade gleamed as it came up and out of her mouth. Berlin jumped as the blade quickly slid across his throat. From the loud yell from Berlin, Tee-Mason burst through the door only to be met by a barrage of bullets let off by the gun of Breana.

Tee fell to the ground with a hole masquerading as his chest. Charlie was quick to pick up the slack, with his Simese burners at full blaze, Breana quickly folded to their blind rage. Charlie check Breana, he then quickly made his way to Berlin's bed. He gave a sorrowful sigh from deep within his lungs. Berlin laid dead, choked on his own blood.

Back here in Westgate, Shay's Point was now under siege, my thoughts were militant the nearer the sound of bullets coming closer, things went silent. Shhh!!! Here they come. Sirens were heard singing that same sad melody. I heard footsteps running away towards the exist of the club. Some more shots were fired, I remained chilling at my desk.

In all the ruckus, I heard Johnson's voice. From this I knew the club was clear, and that my people was being arrested on illegal possession of firearms. Johnson had this superior smirk.

"Black you and you're people, better have papers for these weapons." Johnson says, I smiled, as I reached for my half smoked Queen's cigar in the ashtray. Once I got it to my lips I slowly lit it. I took one long pull of my cigar and pulled out of a drawer, papers for all of my peoples. Johnson looked the papers over, his sweaty brow was beaded up in a heated dismay.

Johnson literally threw the papers back in my face. I leaned back in my leather chair. I picked up the phone. It rang three times before it was picked up on the other end.

"Candy". Candy says over the phone her voice was sweet and refreshingly unexhausted.

"Yo, my peoples have been locked up. Candy send one of your girls to get them out. I'll reimburse you personally." I said to an ever breathing Candy.

"Right Black, I'll see you baby, I'm out." Candy says then hangs up. I reach into the bottom left drawer of my desk, and grab my fifth of Biccardi Dark and slowly raise up out of my chair. I slid to the back exit, my mind deep in thought.

Henry Vereen IV

PART II

Henry Vereen IV

HELLGATE

Marinating in this elixer, thoughts as heated as this Bacardi Dark. I'm drinking. Rain was tickling the brim of my derby, as I slowly strolled to my red Hummer.

The hollow sounding tap of my cane against the concrete echoed in my ear. I slowly came to a stop, I turn to see what my boy, Shamon Created, as by me the Point will always be running.

Snow was falling, and Carlito Indigo was now back on the streets of New York. Baby Boston of course was by his side, maintaining the heat crossbreeding the winter months. As Carlito and Boston was standing on the snow covered sidewalk. A slick 740 IL Beemer pulls up. Out of the Beemer steps sixty and out the passenger side London.

Baby, Boston smiles at her familia as she thought she wouldn't see them again.

"Where's James and Jaisen?" Carlito asks Sixty whom just shrugged his shoulders.

"They're in the Bronx collecting, they'll be back around six AM." London says, speaking up before Carlito lost his cool.

"Yea, Deon's having a party in Westgate, it'll get y'all away from some of the heat here, the plane tickets are at your place." Sixty says to a listening Carlito. Everyone was now getting into the Beemer, their destination, Deon's place.

*   *   *   *

Here in Westgate, Rush and myself was engulfed in a deep conversation.

"I'm saying now that Berlin's dead the west coast is wide open. And that shit with BaiRute, because of him our street value is shaky." Rush says, in his voice I could hear his annoyance. For Rush that was very seldom.

"Rush you need to relax baby boy, in San Francisco I'm going to establish you there to run the operation. BaiRute, the only way to make that fool happy is to give him New York." I said to Rush, whom cut me a curious look with his chinky eyes.

"New York, how the hell are you going to swing New York in your favor?" rush says, sincerely amused, he was intrigued by the idea. I took a pull off of my Queen cigar before I answered Rush's question.

"Carlito's coming out here for his brothers party we're going to swing a deal with him." Rush just smiled at my words.

"For real, didn't Shamon drop his nigga, Quick, in their house." Rush says, truly enjoying himself, but he had a point. BaiRute, I won a close fight with him once I'll do it again. Meanwhile at Shay's Point business was about to start for the night. I left Mojo in charge until I got back there.

Outside the club a black Lincoln sat in the lot, a van was parked in front of it. Inside the cars people was loading their guns. In the van Kerosene was in ample supply. Inside the club, business was rolling for three strong hours. Mojo was keeping a close eye on everything, the splurging of liquor was in its own rights respectable.

Outside, the van and black Lincoln occupants emptied their cars. Moving like apparitions, they swiftly made their way across the street to the club's entrance. Shotguns ripped the torso out of the doorman. Seven men ran in, Shay's Point turned into a shooting range. Two men doused the place with gasoline.

Mojo with no choice, retreated with the rest of my people. A few matches and Shay's Point went up in flames. As Rush pulled up in front of Shay's Point my mind for a split instance went blank. As I watched Shamon's dream, and my promise go up in smoke. Rush sat silent now knowing what to say.

I took a long pull off my Queen cigar and then told Rush to take me home.

*　　*　　*　　*

24

It's been done, my boys done burned that nigga out baby."
Ron Plato says into the phone's receiver, his Texas drawl laced
with excitement.

"Good maybe he'll bow out gracefully and turn the
operation over to us now." Crusian says through a wicked grin.

*   *   *   *

Sixty pulls to a stop in front of Deon's place on Prince
Street. Snow was just starting to fall again as Carlito stepped
out the Beemer and onto the snow covered concrete. The
Beemer slowly pulls off. Carlito slowly makes his way up
Deon's steep stairs. Carlito knocked on the door three times,
Kia, Deon's wife answers the door.

Carlito slowly glanced over this ebony empress, he shook
his head, with a slight grin, he sighed. In Carlito's eyes lust
appeared.

"Yo, let me speak to Deon right fast Shortie". Carlito says
quickly.

"Alright, but make it quick my nigga, he got shit to do. Kia
says trying to conceal her contempt for Carlito. Carlito breezed
by Kia, and on into the living room, where Deon was putting the
finishing touches on a freshly rolled blunt.

"Oh shit, my nigga wadd up. When you get out?" Deon
says as he and Carlito trade handshakes.

"Yo, I need to know something. While I was in, I ran into
Jay, he says y'all caught heat by Ashton." Carlito says, cutting
to the chase of his visit.

"Yea, someone dropped dime, no generals and shit, it had to
be a worker. I'm working or the slow leak as we speak." Deon
says then pauses as Kia walks into the room. The look she gave
Deon made'm shake his head.

"What?" Deon says, not trying to feel Kia at the moment.
Kia just turned and left the room "She's still made because you

fucked her sister, son, then you disowned the child. that was foul son. But anyway, don't worry about the police, we still have the smoothest operation on the eastern seaboard." Deon says then smiles, he hands Carlito the blunt, once lit, the blunt sizzled like the two brothers minds.

*   *   *   *

Brandy's place was ablaze with Sativa, as her and Kavasia was caught in a moment of pleasurable lust. Brandy let out one more dizzy scream as she collapsed in the moment. Kavasia fresh off the hit of Shay's point, was feeling good as he relit the half blunt that sat in the ash tray.

Brandy's phone ringing broke the mood. Brandy quickly picks up.

"Hello." Brandy says, her voice still weak from all the sex.

"Brandy, someone burned down Shay's Point, meet me at Black's place." Mojo says then hangs up. Brandy's high now blown. She looked at Kavasia, she remembered him smelling like gasoline when he got to her place. Brandy's temper was at it's peak. She walked over to Kavasia and smacked the blunt out of his mouth.

Kavasia just looked at Brandy then he smiled, he just got dressed and then showed himself the door. Brandy had plenty to think about. She knew if I or Mojo found out she was sexing with Kavasia, in being skeptical the man who killed Duquine.

Back at my place, the tension was integrated by mental aggression. I sat alone, my Queen cigar simmering in my left hand, Bicardi dark liquefying my right. On the couch sat Charlie Ave, Supreme and Majestic. Standing around Mojo, and Korlane, with Rush standing too, the whole click was present except for Brandy.

"What the deal Black, you know who did it? Let's ice them niggas man." Rush says, the paradox of Rush's words brought a slow smile to my face.

26

"Yea, this shit is getting old, so check it here's the deal." I said as I started to lay out my plan.

Club Isis - Deon's Party

"Welcome to Club Isis, a private party, no invitation, no entry. If ya don't have one fuck you and your people!" The doorman shouts at people trying to get in. Deon's party was in full swing. Myself and Rush occupied a table, dimly lit in the back.

We watched as the lights went dim, then Britney strutted onto the stage behind her two more dancers slowly swayed out as well. The club was ecstatic, Benjamin's and Franklin's were going to see some bare flesh tonight. The Bicardi Dark, I was sipping, held back the tension I was suppressing from last night's events.

Brittany played the stage like a violin, every string on her well curved body slowly came off. As this was happening. I had sent Rush to invite Carlito over to my table. Carlito quickly, out of consideration, accepted my invitation. The crowd erupted when Brittany's 'g' string came off she got close to the edge of the stage.

In front of Deon, Brittany spread her legs, Deon quickly slipped a twenty into her moist box. Brittany shivered, then spazed out coming right on the stage. Once again the crowd around the stage went crazy. Carlito was finally now at my table.

"First off I want to say, I hope there's no hard feelings about what happened between Shamon and Quick." I say to a stern faced Carlito.

"None at all, what's the deal son?" Carlito says, off his vibe, Rush was feeling ancy, the scent of aggression was aggravating the situation.

"My people tell me you run the swiftest operation in New York." I say to ease Carlito's mind off my intentions.

"I'm saying you push more shit, or just about as much shit, as my whole operation does in a week." I continued only to be cut off by Carlito.

"Let me see, you want me to join you. You want to acquire my services." Carlito says to me with a smug look on his face. From this I see why Shamon didn't care for the man.

"Whatever, you keep bullshitting and um Ashton will take your punk ass out. So yea, I want to acquire your service," I say, trying to be indirectly abrasive.

"Shamon didn't tell you about me and partners." Carlito says then pauses. "I don't have any, if you want New York come holler at me." Carlito says then abruptly leaves the table. Rush was shaking his head in a frustrated amusement. I just sipped on my Bicardi Dark, and enjoyed the rest of the show.

Midnight the LAX on a flight arriving from Westgate Charlie Avenue and his entourage finally set down in California. The cool arid air caressing L.A. was a far cry from the freezing temps in Westgate. Once they passed the luggage claim, the three jet- lagged men made their way to the front of the busy airport.

"Where's the contact?" Supreme snaps, his words short and quick.

"Traiman, Black told me he was to pick us up and take us to San Fran." Charlie says fielding the question like a politician. The three men though weary kept their cool - as they waited patiently for their contact to arrive.

*   *   *   *

Rain was washing the streets of New York, steam arose from the heated concrete. A war was about to start brewing, parties involve would evolve rapidly at the repercussion of a tragic expedition.

"Yo, we need to find out who this leak is son, either that or shut Ashton up." Sixty says to London, who was slowly pulling

28

on his backwood. London didn't respond until he let the smoke go.

"Shut Ashton up, and we'll be hunted down by every crooked cop from here to Atlantic City." London says, in a dry sarcastic tone. Sixty shook his head at their dilemma. Pulling to a stop at the light. Pulling up behind them was James and Jaisen Hill.

"We should get one of those niggas to do it." Sixty says referring to James and Jaisen. London just smiled. Looking in the rearview window, James and Jaisen awaited the car to pull off. When the four of them realized whom the other was they pulled over and started to talk amongst themselves.

*   *   *   *

Carlito Indigo and Deon was talking about their situation in grave detail.

"Damn first Ashton then Black, ain't this a bitch?" Deon says pausing for a moment, just to catch a glimpse of a somber Carlito. "I'm saying, we ain't got to deal with Black, but Ashton's another story." Deon finally finishes.

"When we get back to New York, Ashton won't be a problem no more." Carlito says ending the brief conversation.

*   *   *   *

Snow was adrift in downtown Manhattan, a blitz was about to occur, this the beginning of the end for detective Ashton's persuasiveness, for Carlito to see his point of view, the spot, the lab for Carlito's drugs makeup. Inside Sixty was supervising the scene, the only general there, Sixty was risking being caught.

Taking one last look, Ashton signaled his men, the blitz was on. Three men kicked the door in, as the hinges cringed to the force, a shotgun was ripping the closet man to the door. Ashton put a bullet into Sixty's chest, Ashton's men murdered everything, bagged the drugs and abruptly left.

Ashton glanced at Sixty whom lay silently in a dark corner, and a venting smile spreaded across Ashton's pale face. On this critical note, Carlito was in a fix, it played in my favor. BaiRute was about to come into this picture, this brother I couldn't get rid of, even though he recently flipped on me, I still wanted him and Carlito to run New York.

Out in San Fran Charlie was laying low. Majestic and Supreme was keeping a watchful eye on every move Crusian made in San Fran. This was their duty until I arrived in San Francisco. Supreme was about to pull off when some of Crusian's men stopped him. Supreme just punched the gas knocking the man momentarily off his balance.

A car pulled up and screeched to a holt. The man quickly jumped in, Majestic was ready to fire but the sound of the police diverted his attention. Crusian's men quickly eased in their pursuit, and let the police pursue Supreme and Majestic.

*   *   *   *

A slight drizzle tickled Rush's derby as he made his way to an obscure phone booth on Poes Street. The ease in every step Rush took, was relaxed in a calm infuriation. Rush reached into his coat pocket and slowly pulled out a number. Now sliding back the glass door to the booth, Rush then slowly reached for the phone. Rush quickly dials the number, it rang four times before someone picked up.

"Crusian here." Crusian answers, knowing that only his people has this number. Rush smiled to himself as he thought about my plan.

"What's the deal son, this Rush, that shit with Shay's Point was smooth yo." Rush says excited, Crusian paid little attention to the comment.

"So what's Black's next move, is he going to bow out?" Crusian says, in his business oriented mind, that was his most inquisitive question. Rush smiled devilishly to himself. So Rush told'em. Meanwhile on the Island, BaiRute and his people were about to head down to New York City and be my informant in Carlito's escalating situation.

"Yo, Black. I'm saying if we snuff Ashton out, Carlito's not going to swing" BaiRute says. I took a silent heed to his advice.

"Just handle Ashton, Carlito won't be a problem afterwards". I say to a listening BaiRute, whom just hung up on me after that. On my end, the misty rain covered my window, the pieces of my plan is in place, now what's left is to set then in motion. There was a sudden knock on my door.

Once I opened the door, an ampted Rush was standing there.

"Everything's ready, we'll be in the car waiting for you". Rush says, then heads back to the silver gray Jaguar. I just turned and went to the corner where my bags were sitting then I was on my way, to the sun of Texas, and Ron Plato. Meanwhile in Redhook, James and Jaisen was standing over London's dead body.

"What the fuck happened to him, I know he didn't get caught slipping." James says to his quiet brother.

"Who sent him out here?" Jaisen asks, Monty whom informed them of London's dead body, shrugged his shoulders.

"Dunno, but he's one dead nigga." The country Monty says through a whiny voice. James and Jaisen left London's body where it lay. On this note New York was about to be set with blood. Back in Manhattan, Carlito was trying to digest the news about Sixty's death.

"Ashton!, Yea we about to ice that muthafucka." Carlito says, pacing the floor it his flat. Deon shook his head in disgust.

"Calm down Carlito, we don't need you acting crazy dog. Lay low for a moment, I'll have it handled." Deon's words had little effect of Carlito's mind set, the murder of one of their best generals spun Carlito's mind. The phone rang twice, before it was heard by anyone.

"Yea, who dis?" Deon says, his mind reflecting his words, as sheer ice.

"This Jaisen, London's dead. We just found him in Redhook". Jaisen says, cutting to the chase for the phone call. Deon was surprised, usually London wouldn't be one to get caught slipping. These deaths left the air around Deon's operation uncommon. Deon shook his head in disgust.

"Damn, you and James round up everybody and meet up here tonight.' Deon says then hangs up the phone.

*   *   *   *

Texas, flooded by memories of Mexico, I was ancy for the second time in my life. Sun rays blazed my derby, as the grass felt weird underneath my boots, its a lot softer than the grass in Westgate. Ron Plato's whole ranch made my mind race, the way everything seemed to be in existence as one, but this shit is going to be over soon.

Being the shark that I am, I peeped out Ron's snake eye while he looked over my crew as we chatted.

"Black let me say I hate what happened to Shay's Point." Ron says, in his mind laughing at me with sincere contempt. My general idea of him being behind that burning was now solidified.

"Thank you, but is not your fault, its not like you lit the match." I said, I glanced at Kavasia, whom at the moment could barely hold a straight face. Ron's ranch wasn't the spot to provoke him, so to bide my time I just chilled. In the nearby city of Dallas, Ron's new headquarters. Chill and Rolin two of Leroy's boys was now in town.

They were scooping out two of Ron's informers. They parlayed in the cut, then followed the two men to the Parisa Hotel downtown. They waited till the men parked in the parking garage. Chill and Rolin pulled up behind the two men, with silent pistols, Rolin exits the car, a full barrage of bullets, let of by Rolin left the car and occupants stale.

Rolin quickly but calmly made his way back to the car and like ghosts Chill and Rolin disappeared.

*　　*　　*　　*

"Traimen what's the deal with Black, why the fuck are we here." Charlie asks a chilling Traimen.

You're just here to figure out Crusians moves, you got dime on most of 'em. From here out you and your boys lay low, enjoy the sights. Black will be here in about two days, he'll fill in the rest for you.' Traimen says to a nonchalant Charlie. This is why I like Traimen he was a true field General.

*　　*　　*　　*

Paradise, the hold up spot for Deon and company, was jumping. The small club could hold merely over a hundred people. In the back of the club, down along straight hallway, was Baby Boston's office. Deon, Carlito, James, and Jaisen was all in presence. And in the open club BaiRute and his people walked in on the scene.

Their presence radiated, their infamous Island Reps followed them like lost spirits. The bar tenders made a quick call to Boston's office. Shortly Jaisen by himself was out into the club. James and Carlito took up quiet positions over by the bar. Jaisen the coolest of all of Carlito's crew, was now on his way over to BaiRute's table.

"What's the deal baby I ain't seen you in a minute." Jaisen says to BaiRute, showing him love through a handshake. Carlos and Tate looked on.

"I'm saying son, what's the shit, Carlito here?" BaiRute says in one swift breath. Jaisen smiled and then gestured for

BaiRute to follow him. On the outside of the club Ashton's people was set to blitz again, his tactics was meant to make Carlito's business look bad. With a wave of the hand the blitz was on.

Once through the door, broads started screaming, fellas was using each other for human shields. Tear gas, set the club ablaze with a choking sensation. Tate and Carlos pulled their heat and started to rip. Their bullets hunted down the police, James and Jaisen soon joined the fire fight.

Ashton took two to the chest, he immediately called his men back. He wasn't suspecting to get a fight, breathing heavy, Ashton ran out the paradise panting. His heart was racing due to exhilaration. Only five of Ashton's men made it out, they were all bleeding and surprised, they quickly fled the scene.

Carlito has now gained an ally in the fight against Ashton. Deon just smiles to himself, wondering what BaiRute's angle, he was going to let it play out, and held an ace up his sleeve.

*   *   *   *

Kavasia was now showing us around the ranch, of course courtesy of our host. While we were touring the ranch, Plato was on the phone, telling the police what hotel I was staying in, and when I would be back there. Ron didn't know his people whom informed him were dead, and we've by now have switched hotels.

For the first time in a week, a smile crossed my grill. I turned to Rush, whom followed slowly off to my left.

"Rush, send Reese a plane ticket, tell 'em its on me." I told Rush, whom knew what I was talking about. Once we were back on the patio, Ron had a tray of drinks ready. The afternoon hours slowly gave way to evening hours. As the sun went down, the heat captivated the night.

"Black, I hope we can do this again, its been nice my nigga."
Ron says, in his words I could hear a snake hiss in every
syllable. A forced smile crossed my face.

"Yea, we'll see each other again soon, very soon." I say as I
extended my hand to give him a handshake. After this we went
about our business. The ride back to the new hotel was swift.
Korlane was there waiting on us.

"The guns are ready, anytime you want Black." Korlane
says then glances at the Suburban, parked across from the
rooms.

*   *   *   *

"A raid in the late afternoon, what kind of shit was that?"
Deon says to a laughing BaiRute, whom was holding a glass of
Remy.

"I'm saying though they went for it." BaiRute says, then
glances at Baby Boston whom was now approaching them.
BaiRute sized Boston up. Her green contacts flowing with her
silky smooth skin. BaiRute was once again hooked, even though
Boston was smart, BaiRute was known for his thuggish appeal,
leaving broads weak in the heart.

BaiRute was calm, with his blunt smoking Cousin Carlos by
his side he had nothing to worry about. Over by the bar Carlito
and Jaisen was conversing.

"What's this niggas story?" Carlito says, to a smiling Jaisen.

"Yo, this nigga was part of a gang back on the Island named
the Devils. He was the left hand man or right etc. The gang
split up and went to war with each other, this nigga wiped the
whole other gang out, then vanished like a fucking ghost."
Jaisen says then pauses, after taking a sip of his tea colored
liquor he continued.

"I'm saying, that bullshit made'em a legend, the niggas only
twenty-two, and got more props than the fucking President".
Carlito had little to say after Jaisen's explanation, but somehow

Carlito knew I had something to do with BaiRute being there. Carlito took in a deep breath, and let it go, as he peered at Deon.

Carlito didn't like the smell of things, raids in the middle of the day, both his generals dead in a week. Carlito was close but at the same time far from figuring it out. Back at Ron Plato's ranch, a party was brewing.

On the coffee table in the den, coke was being lined up by a razor blade by Kavasia. Ron was up first, as he placed the straw gently toward the opening of his nostril, and with a steady inhaling motion pulled up the coke in a blur.

The phone ringing stung Kavasia's ears before he picked up the chirping phone.

"Yea." Kavasia says, trying to concentrate, because of his high and a broad pulling down his zipper, that was a little hard to do.

"Yea, this Lenny, some of our people was found dead in the parking garage of the Parisa. The same spot where Black is holding up." Lenny says in an almost whisper, now awaiting a response, he listened for it patiently.

"Damn, Lenny get over here quick and bring the boys with you." Kavasia says, his high now blown, he alerted Ron to the situation. After his conversation with Lenny he knew something was wrong. Now doubling back, we were coming full strength on the tilt. Guns, being cocked and silencers being placed, was the only noise fitting the quiet void of the ride.

We finally pulled alongside of Plato's ranch's rear entry. My people filed form the car like well-trained troops. In a blur, like the first seconds of an ambush it was mostly over. With my cane in hand I slowly made my way over to Rush's position, where Ron Plato was laying alongside a slain Kavasia.

I glanced at Mojo, whom handed me his piece. I could feel the heat, the steal chemistry in my palm as I griped it. I raised the gun slowly.

"Black, Black," Ron says gasping for breath, in his final minutes he was going to beg. Shameful chump, his begging was fueling my hatred. "It wasn't me, it was Crusian, it was all his doing. Berlin, BaiRute all his doing." Ron says, a sweat pours in streams down his cheeks. I saw the flames of Shay's Point reflecting in his eyes.

Everything went silent, the gun burst with open rage, the first bullet hit his dome, killing his physical being. The gun bursts two more times, these two bullets aimed for the heart to kill his soul. Rush quickly cleared everyone out, we were on our way to the airport. Korlane left the tickets there for us, the ride there, no one spoke, we still had a long journey ahead of us.

I intend on enjoying the sights, and things in San Francisco.

Daylight broke across New York, BaiRute and his team was up early. Tate was on the phone with Ashton, setting up a date with him to meet. BaiRute was to shoot a bribe to Ashton, whom I was hoping he would turn the 2.4 million down and go green eyed. BaiRute was purposely seducing the beautiful Baby Boston, just to skim for information.

Boston was smooth, BaiRute was sharp with his words, leaving Boston's mind wet with linguistical images. Boston smiled and then with an iniquitous inkling, she let him know to come home with her. A new plot was brewing, the main source was Carlito. Keeping an eye on the situation, was James and Jaisen whom followed Boston and BaiRute's progress.

On the other side of town, I was on the phone with Tate.

"Yo, I don't know if he's going to go for this shit." Tate says lowly, in his voice he didn't want Ashton to. It sounded as if he knew what I was planning. If so he was sharper than I thought.

"BaiRute knows what the deal is, if he don't accept the bribe." I told 'em, on the other end I could picture the smile on Tate's face. This brother had a fetish for violence, Tate hung up without saying anything further. While cruising in a Benz recently copped by Carlos. Kingsmon and Kremone were enjoying the atmosphere of Manhattan.

"Dog, can you smell it? Kingsmon asks a relaxed Kremone. Kremone smirked as his thoughts slipped into place.

"Yea, its thick right, but the scent." Kremone says, his smirk now a wide grin, "but the scent," he repeats.

"Its like the most beautiful type of tension, ya hear me, money shits beautiful" Kingsmon smirks, as Kremone is now laughing at his own words.

The cellular phone ringing brought the two out of their laughing.

"Yea." Kingsmon says quickly.

"Yo, this BaiRute baby, check it out. I need ya'll to drop me off somewhere. So met me here at the hotel." BaiRute says then hangs up.

Four PM, mid town Manhattan, Ashton was awaiting BaiRute and his people. On cue, a sleek Benz carrying BaiRute and his entourage pulls up. Ashton eyed BaiRute and his people as they approached. Carlos held a small briefcase, the obvious bribe. Tate was holding a general expression of anxiety.

Tate wasn't nervous, but he wasn't going to hold nothing back if something went wrong. Once face to face, BaiRute and Ashton both traded snakish grins.

"2.4 that's the deal, right". Ashton says as the smile on his face dissipates.

BaiRute's smile became an icy expression.

"You accepting?" BaiRute says cutting to the point. Ashton sighed.

"What's the condition of this bribe?" Ashton says, in his thoughts he was just amusing himself.

"You leave Carlito and his people alone, and that is it." BaiRute says, his face now a frown because of Ashton's sudden laughter.

"2.4 million. When I could have just as much and more by getting a piece of the action." Ashton says, "Baby boy, maybe when you get some business sense, this'll make a lot more sense to you." On that note Ashton walked away from the meeting. Tate of all people was smiling.

"Yo, that muthafucka done put verbal on you son." Carlos says to a now quiet BaiRute, not quiet because of Ashton's words, but because he knew he would be able to lash back in a very short minute.

*   *   *   *

Several Days Earlier

Redhook the infamous section of Brooklyn, London was there checking his people. On the solo, rare even for a Redhook veteran, London was true to his own way. These streets taught him James and Jaisen Hill how to play the game. London quickly made his way to Breeze's house. Breeze was a stool pigeon for Carlito he kept the crew informed.

Breeze was standing on his stoop in front of his place seemingly awaiting London's arrival. The two smiled and gave each other dap.

"My nigga, what's the deal? I know its some shit if ol London comes by." Breeze says with a sincere rugged smile.

"No doubt, check this. We got a leak, and if we don't get this fool we all going up baby." London says to a now thinking Breeze slowly stroking his chin.

"Yo, I heard about that, No one knows who the muthafucka is." Breeze says, then briefly hesitates before speaking again.

"I'm saying though, what's your thoughts on this shit?" Breeze asks London as if he's now fishing for answers. London thought for a moment.

"It's got to be someone on the inside, but everyone in this click is too tight for that." London says to a head shaking Breeze.

"I think you got that shit son. In cases like these son, the answer be right there staring you in the face and shit. Ya feel me. Keep ya friends even closer in this one baby." Breeze says to an agreeing London.

"Alright, money I'm out." London says, then gives Breeze some dap then made his way to his car. Now getting back to the present time, BaiRute was over at Boston's place, a night cap was the suggested way to spend the evening. Outside of Boston's place parked on the street were Kingsmon and Kremone. BaiRute had a suspicion that Boston was setting him up, so he asked Kingsmon and them to watch his back.

A slight misty rain collected on the Benz's windshield, as Kingsmon and Kremone sat in silence. A thick cloud of Sativa hung over them in a still motion. Holding their toolies in their laps they both kept an lazy eye on the street. On the inside of Boston's apartment, BaiRute was enjoying his exploration of Boston, hands roaming, kissing the body of this sweet chocolate.

BaiRute gave an exhilberated sigh, as he slowly rolled off of Boston's sweat soaked body. BaiRute was loving the friction, the dual of the mind struggle for New York's drug games in the shadow. BaiRute smiled to himself, he hasn't been in this situation in a good minute, and couldn't wait for it to get thick. Boston glanced at the time awaiting James and Jaisen to show.

Back outside, a red Range pulled up and slowly comes to a stop. The rain was almost in a full drizzle, Kingsmon and Kremone peered out through their smokey windows. Out of the Range jumps James and Jaisen, on the other side of the street. The Benz's doors open, smoke rose out the car like steam. Kremone let the first bullet loose, shattering the passenger side window, inches away from James' head.

Up in Boston's window, BaiRute was peering out with an intense glare. Boston was easing close to her gun. BaiRute dressed with haste. He took one step backwards, with his guard unconsciencly down, he turned and found himself staring down a cold black barrel.

"Who you working for? We know about the bribe my nigga." Boston says, her eyes affixed on BaiRute's dome, her target. BaiRute froze for a moment, accessing the situation.

"I'm working for your people, and how did you find out about the bribe." BaiRute says sharply. Boston pauses for a moment not realizing the implications of BaiRute's words. BaiRute took advantage of Boston's hesitation, he snatched the gun from her quickly, and then viciously slapped Boston, spinning her to the floor.

Quickly BaiRute fled Boston's apartment, the tenants could be heard hustling inside their apartments looking for cover, as BaiRute ran by their doors. Outside Jaisen grabs his brother James whom took several bullets to the chest. Jaisen threw his brother in the car, then quickly jumped in the driver seat, and spun off in a flurry.

While smoke was drifting up as the tires spun most rapidly on the range. Kingsmon and Kremone ceased fire, BaiRute suddenly submerges out of the apartment building, splashing in a mixture of a blood and rain puddle. He quickly ran toward Kingsmon and Kremone the three made a hasty retreat, as they also fled the scene.

Back in the range James was slightly breathing, Jaisen drove furiously trying to get to a hospital. His vision blurred by the rain, and tears that started to form in his eyes. James drew his final breath and slowly slipped away. Jaisen felt this, and he then stopped the car, with tears running in streams down his face, Jaisen exited the car, and slowly walked away in the opposite direction.

Meanwhile, at the S.F.O. Airport in San Francisco me and my people was being picked up by a two car caravan. Traimen and his people were sharp, if you wanted standard help, by me being sharp in your thoughts and actions, was a necessary necessity. The sun was beaming radiantly with a flare for brilliant heat, it sent chills down my spine.

Once in the car, I rode shotgun with a quiet Traimen. I scanned his facial expression, he was relaxed, typical for a Cali nigga. He was the only one in my operation to eerily remind me of myself. I pulled out one of my Queen Cigars, and lit it up, I took one large pull, once I let the smoke go, I broke the icy silence between us.

"You kept tabs on Reese?" I asked, only to satisfy my curiosity. Traimen's eyes stayed on the rode as he decided to answer my question.

"Yea, he's in a local hotel. I was going to let the man chill at my flat, but Charlie and them advised me against that." Traimen says, his words flowing in that West coast coolness. A little later we pulled up to Traimen's place in Jonesburgh, a town on the outskirts of San Fran.

The atmosphere around my people was uneasy, for some their first time ever on the west coast. The heated climate, the chemistry of my team was fluent. It's time to start the final leg of my plan. Rush slipped away from the crowd, he pulled his cell phone and dialed a quick seven. The other line picked up after ringing twice.

"Crusian." Crusian says, his voice and mind distorted by the coke flowing through his veins.

"What the deal, son. We're here now, shits going to plan, be ready for us," Rush paused, feeling a brief premonition, "Crusian, dog I'm warning you don't fuck me over, it's your life if you do, so don't fuck with me." Crusian laughed at Rushes threat, Crusian should of took heed to it. Betrayal in this business is nothing new, but to cross Rush, was to seal your fate.

With Rush being from San Fran, that worked meticulously in my favor that would be proven in the long run. A few hours went by and I once again with my people, rebriefed them of my plan.

* * * *

Going back to when London was still breathing, he was on his way to meet up with his brethren in Uptown Manhattan. He drove with his window halfway down, letting an icy breeze caress his narrow face. His thoughts like magnetism, was slowly coming to a conclusion of whom the snitch was. He drove steadily letting his mind drift.

Later, London pulled to a stop in front of a small diner, a low key spot for him, something of an escape to get away from it all. Once inside, he headed for a table in the back. James and Jaisen were their occupying the table. Smiles broke out around the table, as the crew members gave each other dap, as family recognition.

"What's the deal my nigga?" Jaisen says, realizing London's perplexed facial expression. London forced a smirk, from this Jaisen knew his long term friend was feeling something arid.

"Yo, I just spoke to Breeze. That nigga thinks its someone in the click. And you know, when that nigga ain't heard nothing something's wrong." London says, his words left his brethren temporarily wordless.

"So who you think it is, this bullshit is shorting my money." James says, his tone almost subliminal, as James words hung in London's subconscience.

"At this point who the fuck knows, yo have anybody heard from Sixty." The reply he got was an uneasy no. London seeing where this conversation was leading he decided to drop the matter until the next day.

*   *   *   *

As the night fell is San Fran, the heat remained as an constant, electrifying the nocturnal atmosphere. Myself Rush, and Mojo was invited for a late night cruise on Crusian's yacht. Once there I was astounded, the boat was smooth, as most boats where white, Crusians boat was a pure black marble color. The windows surrounding the lounge area was mirror tinted.

The furniture in the lounge area, were made of the finest Corinthian leather. After Crusian greeted us, we were offered drinks.

"Vodka, Grapefruit?" Crusian asks me with a sly grin, that gripped his square check bones. I glanced at him sheerly before I spoke.

"Dark on Crush diamonds," I retorted, trying to conceal my contempt for the man. While we sipped on our drinks the boat pulled away from the darken docks. Before the real conversation got started, I began to smoke on my cigar once again. Crusian, was studying my motions, as in trying to figure how did a nigga come by so much status.

"Alright, enough bullshit," Crusian blurts, piercing the elegant silence.

"What's on your mind Crusian?" I asked, as I looked at him, I could see the match that set Shays Point ablaze.

"When Berlin suggested that I expand my business, with him, I thought he was joking. But as time went on, I saw grave potential in the arrangement." Crusian says, now I know my throat was on the line. Rush and Mojo traded looks as they were struck to hold their composure "Berlin and R-."

"Yes, I know," Crusian says once he cuts me off. "You sent temptation to Berlin's door, and its probable that you did Ron yourself." I was amused, at how he could surmise all of my actions, but didn't now what I had in store for him.

"Yea, I've enjoyed doing business with you," Rush cut me a short look, reminiscent of the one, after my talk with Carlito in Club Isis. Rush was laughing on the inside, his expression amused at the sarcasm echoing in my voice.

"Yes, I'd presume you would. It's good to finely meet the man who put this all together, of course you're boy Shamon, may he rest in peace." Crusian's words, especially the use of Shamon's name was meant to erk me. That they indeed did, but I couldn't show my infuriation. I took a long pull off my Queen cigar, purposely ending the conversation.

The cruise came to an end as we then got back into the renta-cars. The drive back to Jonesburgh was swift and quiet. In the speakers adrenaline performed by Mobb Deep was blaring. I needed to hear something sincerely grimmy, to ease my rage, something about this beat is calmly provoking.

Back at Crusian's yacht, Crusian was on the phone with Johnson in Westgate, dropping dime on a drug shipment to my newly routed business at Club Isis.

"Who is this?" Johnson asks, his wispy voice now acute, paying close attention.

"A friend, a very close friend." Crusian says, his voice as sharp as an icepick.

"Don't fuck with me, if this is a prank." Johnson says but is cut off.

"The fuck, a prank I'm giving you Black, you stupid fuck!" Crusian says, abruptly and then hung up on a bewildered Johnson. Crusian smiled to himself, he just put a noose around my neck, and I didn't see this one coming.

While in the car, I thought about the brief conversation with Crusian. I found myself taken back, who the fuck did he think he was, that I would give him shit. That picture stung like an unsuspected bitch slap. Most people seem to live their lives being consumed in vengeance. My lust was abstract to the norm, I was getting colder by the second.

I had to be patient, and let my plan follow through to its ending, a long wait was ahead of me.

* * * *

Westgate was covered in an even blanket of snow. Not enough to bring things to a halt, but enough to equify the flow of things. One of my runners, Perry, was awaiting the arrival of the 8 p.m. bus, the last evening bus on the Galpa schedule. The icy breeze kept Perry company, a huge illuminating light came about full circle, as the headlights of the 8 p.m. bus came about full into the terminal.

Unaware of the danger looming, Perry waited for the baggage people to start removing bags, from underneath the bus. Perry with his senses alert, made his way to the luggage. He went trough three bags, before he came across the black duffel bag. The bag was marked with a phony address, with Westgate as its main destination.

Outside the Greyhound station, Johnson was following up his anonymous tip, that he received earlier on. They let Perry collect the shipment, once Perry did so, he then went to his car. His pace was a gliding one, as he covered ground quickly with long flawless strides. Johnson started his car as he awaited for Perry to pull off so that he could tail'em.

The snow was now an icy slush underneath Perry's car tires. Perry felt indifferent dealing with me indirect, all the new faces, he didn't know who to trust. As Perry's thoughts swirled in his mind, Johnson kept a close distance. Johnson was finally going to get some closer. He always resented me after his partners Tolip's death.

Later on, Perry pulls around back to the rear entrance of Club Isis. He froze for a moment before he went into the club, somehow he knew this would be the last time he would see the outside as a free man. Inside the club, it was a meek scene, with the show not really starting until around eleven p.m. A few men sat at tables drinking beer or whatever beverage they desired.

Johnson had his people ready, but he waited a few minutes, just so Perry could be caught arranging the dope. As time slid by some more squad cars converged on the unsuspecting club attendees. On the inside, Perry pulled out several keys of wood, coke, heroin and then in ounces, P.C.P., black velvet, and crystal meth. This shipment alone was worth 16 million on the street.

Johnson checked his watch, he pulled his piece signaled his men, and then they swarmed the club like angry bees. Without a single shot being fired, all of the occupants were now in police custody. Johnson was happy, damn fool, if only he knew then that he'd completely shut me down in Westgate.

Crusian was an old head, but I didn't know he knew that much about me and my past relations with Johnson. This proved to be a chilling blow to me, although I never doubted myself, I felt that I was loosing my grasp on the situation.

*   *   *   *

Manhattan was eerily calm, on Prince Street at Deon's flat, Carlito had his hands full trying to calm an almost irate Jaisen. Deon was sitting in his recliner submerged deep into his own thoughts.

"They going to feel me, ya hear me!" Jaisen says, as he feverishly paced back n forth. "They fucking going to feel me." Jaisen repeats, this bringing Deon back from his mental journey.

"Chill out son, we going to get that faggot ass mothafucka, you just chill till then." Deon says to Jaisen in a re-assuring tone. Although Deon felt funny about trying to comfort one of most prolific killers he's ever known, he checked that as a mental note. He would've told Jaisen not to go that route, but he negated that, James was his brother, Deon decided to run parallel to his usual reasoning.

A knock on Deon's front door, stalled the tension as Carlito opened the door. Boston slid in, even though her face was slightly bruised from BaiRute's slap. Boston's eyes shifted to Jaisen, whom seem to stare at her with pleading eyes. Boston looked away first, as in those eyes she saw London, and Sixty staring back. Her heart skipped a beat, like a broken drum off rhythm.

They all resided in this quietness, taking that always fleeting silent moments. Over on Spring Street, BaiRute was on a payphone with me.

"Black this shit done went backwards, I think a wars about to start. But fuck it, we ready thought." BaiRute unwavered confidence gave me a slight comfort. This was an unsuspecting turn, and I was sure that Ashton would take advantage of the situation.

"You got enough people there, and I'm saying you need anything you can get it." BaiRute wasn't one for long phone conversing, he hung up after my last comment. He looked around, as if he was nervous. BaiRute wasn't with Kingsmon and Kremone, he instead took comfort with the company of his cousin Carlos. Tate was at the entrance of the Manhattan Bridge.

In even breaths, mist flowed, as Tate breathed. He was awaiting Donaven, Les Walls, and Ramone. The reinforcements of BaiRute's crew. A lethal conflict was in the making, and it was BaiRute's time to shine. He would be damned if he came up short this time.

*   *   *   *

Back in Westgate, Janet one of Candy's girls was quickly making her way towards a nearby payphone. The snow was falling in an abstract rhythm, as was the footsteps that Janet took. Once in the booth she quickly found my number and picked up the receiver. She dialed frantically, but smooth. The phone rang twice before I picked up.

"Yea," I said slowly, feeling the effects of the liquefied dark.

"Black, it's me Janet. I got to breeze quick my nigga." Janet says then pauses, listening for a reply, to see if she has my attention.

"Word, what's happen?" I said, now trying to concentrate. From the way Janet's words were snapping, I could tell something has went terribly wrong.

"They got Perry, Club Isis has been shut down, and Candy's no where to be found." I could feel the vibes of panic flowing through Janet's every word. This is twice some dumb shit has happened.

48

"Don't worry about nothing, Candy nor Perry will sing to anybody." Janet laughed a little, surprised at my nonchantles.

"Damn Black, baby they got the element on this one, all I'm saying wherever you at watch your back, and stay there. Fuck Westgate, it's hotter than a muthafucka out here. I'm out my nigga." From Janet, I conceived a visual of the future, it wasn't looking good for my business. With Westgate no longer an option, New York had to become part of the dynasty.

Meanwhile, brooding at his desk in the thirty first precinct, was a contemplating Johnson. Seriously, peeved about Perry's unwillingness to talk, he had the mind to go beat the info out of Perry, that he required. Although shifting his emotions was difficult. Johnson managed to keep his cool. Johnson knew he had me, transporting drugs over state lines made my case a federal offense.

He even made the call to the feds personally. On those thoughts, Johnson's stone expression became a vengeful grin. Johnson awaited the feds with an exuberant eagerness. Johnson was able and willing to give them all the information they needed. They literally blessed Johnson when they gave him consultating status on the case.

Once the feds arrived, they were headed up by Ron Platos paid off, agent, Agent Somerson. They all traded those signature handshakes, they made their way back towards the captain's office for more privacy. Once in the office, the conversation about me began.

"Okay gentleman, let's get to the point. There was a murder down in Texas. His name is Ron Plato, we know he had ties with this new dynasty. Before him the second most member Berlin was also murdered. A woman slit his throat." Agent Somerson says then glances over at Johnson, whom sat with a crude smirk. "The only thing we need to know is where's Black, A.K.A. Anthony Blacmon." On this note, Johnson was now obliged to speak up.

"Anthony Blacmon, he started the dynasty here in Westgate with his now deceased partner Shamon Teller. These kids are not your average drug dealers. Their operation quietly spreads across the nation." Johnson says, then pauses gathering the latest information in his fruitful mind.

"We haven't seen Black in a few days, seems he damned disappeared, but a few hours ago we brought down a piece of his operation, a drug shipment from San Francisco. "My hunch is, that's where he's holding up." Johnson says, then glances back at a smiling Agent Somerson. "I have a request," Johnson says with a sinister smile. "I want to be there when you bust that cocky son of a bitch." Johnson says to an all out agreeing crowd.

Part III

Henry Vereen IV

Spaded Flush

Midnight, a steady flow of freezing rain was caressing the streets of Manhattan. London was on his way to meet Sixty. He was still reflecting on his meeting the night before, with James and Jaisen. London's thoughts were perplexed, he peered through a vast prism of pictures of snitch suspects.

He slowly started dismissing the unlikely suspects, Carlito was out, because he brought news back from the joint of the snitch. Everyone else he was usually around except for Deon. This thought rode London's mind, he was now for certain, all was left was to prove it.

Later, London pulled up to the corner of Spring Street. Right next to Prince Street where Deon's flat is located. On the corner in the freezing rain, was a lone standing Sixty. His umbrellas was a black fixture that suited his thuggish apparel. London pulled to a quick stop. Sixty quickly slides into the passenger seat.

"What's the deal son?" Sixty asks, as he and London give each other some dap.

"Yo, I think I know who this fucking snitch is." London says as he pulls away, headed down Spring Street.

"Who you think it is?" Sixty says his voice radiant with frustration. London realized his thoughts before he spoke.

"I think it's Deon." London says, pausing long enough to catch a glimpse of Sixty's facial expression. "I'm saying," London continues.

"Carlito can't be it, because he's been in Philly for almost a year, him and Boston." London spoke clear and brisk. Sixty sat for a moment in silence, he analyzed what London has said. It was true about Carlito and Boston, but he still doubted that Deon was the snitch.

"Deon! What the fuck son, what's he going to gain outta that shit? How the fuck are you going to prove that?" Sixty says, his mind now racing, in his heart, being fueled by betrayal, hate was growing quickly. The car grew quiet as the two, momentarily soaked in their own thoughts. Once the silence was broken, scheming began to feel the snitch out.

*   *   *   *

James and Jaisen was at home, with some jazz music parlaying in the background, the two brothers were relaxing. The phone rang, and then James picked up.

"Yea." James says, as a statement and not as a question.

"This Deon, James, I need you and Jaisen to get the snitch." Deon says on his end with a sick grin.

"For real who is it?" James asks, his relaxed mood was now quickly dissipating.

"Yo, I found out it was Breeze, he's playing like he doesn't know anything. Since he don't I figure we should shut his ass up for good." Deon says, his smile now a borderline frown. James didn't like the reasoning behind Deon's request, but he quickly dismissed his own feelings. Breeze was his boy, all of them; London, Jaisen, James and Breeze came up together in Redhook.

James hung up on Deon, he then glanced at a blunt smoking Jaisen, he shook his head in disgust. Now secretly wishing he wasn't in this business, but it wasn't personal it was just business, a fucked up piece of business at that. In Redhook, two hours after James' short conversation with Deon, Breeze was at the local corner store. He purchased a Dutch and a fifth of Gin.

Once he paid for it, he slid out the store easily. Once outside he traded a few sly remarks with the usual loiterers. Breeze slowly with a pimps bop walked down his lively street. The weather was cool, a sharp brisk breeze kept Breeze company on what normally would be a short walk back to his crib.

Breeze's thoughts were on the case of the snitch, his pattern of thoughts were as clear as crooked beat cops selling dope, on the neighboring street. Breeze never thought he would be labeled as a snitch, but in dealing with Deon, his third eye should've been wide open. A sudden surge in the chilling breeze brought Breeze back to his senses.

Jaisen and James finally pull up on their home street in Redhook, they spot out Breeze walking rather quickly down the street. James took a deep breath, he checked his silencer, cocked his nine and then nodded at Jaisen to drive. The car quickly made its way up the narrow street. Once up on Breeze, Breeze looked to his left.

He caught eye contact with James, and James didn't waver, he pulled the trigger letting three rounds off. The bullets silently and quickly cut Breeze down. The concrete quickly met Breeze, harshly breaking his fall. James sunk back into the passenger seat, feeling a cold chill vibrate through his heart, he sat silent. Jaisen shook his head in disbelief and calmly drove back to Manhattan.

*   *   *   *

The night sky was clear here in Jonesburgh, you could feel the distant blaze of all the stars shimmering in the vast ebony canvas of the sky. Myself and Rush was out on Traimen's immense front porch, immense as in compared to Chancelor Avenue's front stoops back in Westgate. We were sharing a blackwood and a futuristic conversation.

"Word, this is all its about, family and money. Keep your people rugged and rich, shit we'll always be tight. And always keep your cool, let fools shoot their bluff, hold yours and come with a spaded flush, or a diamond straight or whatever it is, make sure you come sharp." I told Rush, he was pulling down the knowledge as he was letting the backwood smoke go.

After the cloud of smoke vaporized, Rush slowly began to speak.

"I'm feeling that, once this bullshit blow over, the dynasty is going to be even tighter. There's no doubt in my mind, shits going to be grand." Rush says, he then starts to cough, due to not being a deep smoker. Before I could speak my phone was ringing. I picked it up and was wondering was it more bad news.

"Yea, this Black, who dis?" I say, trying to be upbeat.

"This Perry son, they just let me loose on bond. I'm going to go see Candy. Yo, Black they on you kid watch your back son. Let me get off this piece they might of tapped this shit, awright my nigga, I'm out." From the sound of Perry's frustrated voice, Westgate could see one final flare up of my people's rage. Even thought as I sit here and reflect upon all of this, it seems funny all this drama over a couple of hundred million of drug loot.

After my conversation with Perry, he was then on the move to Candy's place. In his car, he stashed his chrome, and was in an array of thoughts. The ism his mind flowed with was simple logic. Once he was caught, Club Isis shut down and Candy ran the place. It was simple, detract the weak link. Candy was that link.

Johnson on the solo, was following Perry anticipating this move. Johnson would need backup if Perry decided to go out in a blaze. Johnson really wanted me, his trip out here to San Fran was already approved by his Captain. To him Perry was just a way to pass time. Slowly Perry pulls onto Green Street, a rather quiet middle class neighborhood.

Perry took a deep breath, as if it were his last. He parked the car on the curb, he grabbed his chrome, he then checked the scene out, after casing the house he would be soon evicting the tenants of, he checked the nine that was finally in place in his draws area.

Perry was cold in his thoughts, knowing that Candy and myself was close, he never conceived the thoughts of killing her until know. Once up on Candy's porch, Perry's mind seemed to clear of unnecessary clutter. He knocked twice on the old worn out screen then rung the doorbell to insure that she would answer. The door slowly opened by a scantily clad. Candy, Perry looked on pleasantly at her well curved figure, with a short shere house coat on, it left little to the imagination.

Candy quickly let Perry in, she pulled at her house coat as it was sliding open revealing her nakedness underneath. Perry paid that no mind as he concentrated on his feverish task. Candy hadn't a clue of what was on Perry's mind. She watched him ease across her living room, and then take a seat on her couch.

With cold black eyes, Perry focused on a somewhat uneased Candy. Perry reached in his coat and pulled his chrome, fear lept into Candy's eyes as her body froze. Perry slowly rose up off of Candy's couch as he slowly raised his pistol. A loud explosion echoed throughout the house, and onto Johnson's ears, whom immediately radioed for backup.

Units in the area converged onto the scene quickly, Perry watched from the front window, one, two, then three squad cars pulled up. Perry, geeked up on his own coldness, pulled his other burner from the inside of his pants. He smiled this harsh grin, stepped over Candy's now lifeless body and opened the front door.

Perry got off a few rounds, before his body was completely infested with lead, as his lifeless body fell to the ground, so did my business in Westgate.

Escaping the escalating heat that was on the rise in Manhattan, BaiRute decided to take his people back to the Island. ON the corner of Charleton Boulevard at the store, parked on the side was Donaven and Tate. They were awaiting Carlos, then they were onto their future destination of Diamond Street, their hold up spot.

The two not knowing of the danger, sitting across the street, was just chilling in the car, listening to the local radio station. Jaisen cocked his two baby oozies, and quickly slid out of the passenger side. His people followed his lead just as quickly. None of BaiRute's people suspected Jaisen to be in the Island, but they know beef in the streets tends to follow you as you travel.

Jaisen let his two burners let off heat, as the first round of bullets scattered through Donaven's and Tate's car. The bullets ripped Tate's right side of his face off, as he lay slumped on a stunned Donaven. Jaisen's next volly of bullets rocked Donaven's car with the force of hate. Donaven jumped out the car and started to spring down Charleton Boulevard.

Jaisen let his third party of bullets loose, Donaven in his fear and panic could hear the bullets whispering his name, as they whistled towards him. The bullets caught the full length of Donaven's back, causing a severe whiplash reaction, in the way Donaven's body jerked inward, and his head snapped back.

Carlos, not wanting to see his death, fled the store through its back entrance. He caught the city bus on nearby Nineteenth Street. He gasped for breath as he tried to calm down, he wouldn't be able to until he got to Diamond Street.

BaiRute sat quietly underneath a thick cloud of Sativa smoke. His thoughts were blazing through his mind at tremendous speeds. After reassessing his plans, troops and guns, BaiRute was now amped up to go back to Manhattan. Kremone's crib was scarcely furnished, but it had sufficed for BaiRute's immediate purposes.

BaiRute's mind drifted to his cousin, Carlos, whom was the last of BaiRute's true bloodline. He wanted to leave Carlos on the Island basically to give himself a piece of mind, but he knew Carlos wouldn't agree. On the thought of Carlos, a knock brought BaiRute's thoughts back. Kremone slid over to the door, leaving his heat on the table next to where he was sitting.

Kremone opened the door to a dismayed Carlos, whom was still panting from the events that happened earlier. BaiRute's high now blown, was mad.

"What the fuck happened to you?" BaiRute says, as he pushed Kremone to the side. Carlos stepped in, before he answered BaiRute's question.

"Yo, Jaisen, showed the fuck up from outta nowhere, then crazy shots went the fuck off. Donaven and Tate is dead yo." Carlos says, Kingsmon and Kremone, and Ramone was all listening. BaiRute's thoughts became militant, he was not for sure, he was going back to Manhattan, with a vengeance on his mind, it was now on.

The guns were oiled and loaded, they were in the back of Kingsmon's car. Everyone was set and ready, the 45 minute drive to Manhattan was about to begin. Meanwhile, on a flight that just left Westgates small airport, Johnson was now on his way out here to San Francisco.

The only thing, that seemed to keep Johnson going, was the thought of me, my head at the end of a gellitines descent. Johnson thought about Tolip's death, the connections of Varia's death. Those thoughts floated on his weary mind constantly. Not being able to put me away was a major beef he carried within.

In Johnson's mind, I was already convicted, and sentenced to death. All that was left was my execution. In a way, I accepted the role of being Westgate's most notorious drug czar ever. Being constantly hounded by Johnson and the entire 31st precinct, it was all a pleasure. Just to see that hard regertated look on Johnson's face.

Johnson with those sharp eyes and stern features, he was determined to see me hang. I was just waiting on him to try once again to catch me. I felt like this ginger bread man, but the outcome would be difficult. As Johnson peered out the plane's window, he was agreeing to himself in silence that he would get closure on a three year old situation.

*   *   *   *

Rush was now on the solo, his mind traveled as he rode around Jonesburgh. He picked up his cell phone, and hit his redial button, which quickly put him through to Crusian's private line. As the phone was ringing on the other end, Rush took those few seconds to gather his thoughts. The other end was finally picked up on.

"Yea." Crusian says, his voice relaxed for a change. Rush smiled to himself. In all this time of being my right-hand, that nigga neva lost his sense of humor.

"Yo, shits good this way, I'm saying Black don't know shit. Since we've been out here, I've gotten him to chill." Rush says just to feel out Crusian's true feelings.

"So what's the deal Rush? Is Black going to come around?" Crusian says, his voice more demanding in tone.

"The fuck you think, that he's going to give it to you that easily. Dog, you'd be better off putting a bullet in that nigga's dome." Rush's response irritated an already insulted Crusian, but Rush could give a fuck less, about Crusian's feelings.

"Maybe I'll just do that." Crusian says, then hangs up. Rush at this moment didn't know about Johnson coming out here with the feds as his reinforcement. On that note Rush was going to flip. But that would be on Crusian.

*   *   *   *

Back to Manhattan, when London was still living a rare meeting between Carlito, Deon, Sixty and London was about to take place, Boston was supposed to attend but was running late. Kia was frustrated she didn't want them there, to her that was the only thing that keep Deon from giving her a full commitment.

Kia in her frustration grabbed her coat and then abruptly headed out the front door. ON her way down the stoop, Kia ran into a slow walking Boston. Kia and Boston never had much to say to each other, but Kia couldn't resist the opportunity.

"You hear to, for another drug gathering, all ya'll need to get out the game. Fuck it, fuck ya'll, the only one I want out the game is Deon." Kia says to a mild mannered Boston.

"Bitch please if it wasn't for these drug gatherings, your ass wouldn't be draped in all that silken linen, and thick chains around your neck, and diamonds around your pretty little ankles." Boston says to the more sensitive and daintier Kia.

"All I want is Deon." Kia says as her eyes become glassy from forming tears. She began to walk away from Boston.

"Damn you whipped, bitch get a life, the only way Deon's getting out the game is by dying out!" Boston says then goes on up and on into Deon's front door. Kia continued on walking, letting the brisk breeze and light rain accompany her. Inside Deon's flat, in his living room they were discussing the Black Velvet that Sixty was developing and the snitch.

Deon took on a pull of the Black Velvet, that was rolled in a gutted backwood. Deon immediately after inhaling began to cough.

"Damn this some good shit. What the fuck you got in this." Deon says in his words, you could feel the dollar signs rising with every syllable. Sixty smiled.

"Come on now, if I told you the ingredients, it looses its mystique and if I don't move this shit, it'll be dead weight, that can't be moved that's how hot this shit is." Sixty says with a certain proudness in his voice.

"Yo, let's get down about the snitch, what's the deal with that?" Carlito asks Deon, whom was finished readjusting himself.

"The snitch has been smoked out, he's a very quiet muthafucka now." Deon says, London and Sixty was surprised, they weren't convinced, it seemed to be convenient. The two traded looks, as their suspicions were confirmed.

"So who was it?" Sixty asks, his voice now an affluent coldness. Deon felt the chill.

"It was Breeze, he was a stooley, he turned on us." Deon studied, Sixty's and London's reactions. London sunk back into his seat. Sixty almost perfectly duplicated London's reactions. It was a blow to London's intelligence as well as Sixty. Neither of them could grasp the idea of Breeze being the snitch.

"Who did'em?" London says, eyes now focused on Deon. Deon felt London's inner rage, but was too savvy to get caught up in that.

"I sent James and Jaisen. The two never miss." Deon says, his intent, to show London who ran the organization. Carlito sat and watched, he felt the arridness forming around the two. Carlito knew London well enough to know when the man would flip. Carlito was witnessing the begining of the end of his crew as he knew it.

Sixty took a long sip of his drink, then dismissed himself from the meeting and Deon's flat. London followed a similar suit. Between Carlito and Deon sat a bewildered Boston. She knew something was wrong, but just couldn't place what.

Ice hung in the atmosphere around them, they sat silently sipping on their mixes, and soaking in abyssal type thought. Boston's thoughts reflected back to London's and Sixty's facial expressions. Their perturbed look, and the contempt in their eyes when they looked at Deon. The future of the crew was looking bleak, Boston couldn't imagine her brethren falling apart, but she knew it was part of the game.

Manhattan looked rather small to London right now. His mind was sick with thoughts of Breeze's death. London blamed himself for not seeing it coming, but he let the guilt subside to the left, letting it marinate into a fine rage. As rain beaded up on his windshield for what seemed like hours of driving, London finally pulls to a stop in front of James' and Jaisen's place.

Once London got to James' and Jaisen's door, those thoughts of why seemed to ring in London's mind. London knocked three times, the door quickly comes open. To London's surprise one of Jaisen's many women was standing there. With a smile, the girl stood there silently. She was slim with long dark and shapely legs, her stomach was exposed, with a six pack ripping through it, and her breast sat firmly in place.

London quickly regained his thoughts, the woman caught his breath, London quickly admitted to himself that this woman was beautiful.

"Yo, where's Jaisen at?" London asks the young lady, London couldn't resist looking her, once more, up and down. The lady pointed towards the back. London stepped by this ebony goddess, and proceeded towards the back. Not showing his frustration, London took his time getting to the back.

Once in the back, London was now witness to an erotic scene. The coffee table was covered in coke, with two broads with straws sniffing lines. Over on the couch another broad was nonchalantly freestyling Jaisen joint. The only odd thing, James was no where around. London shook his head in amazement, London always wondered why Jaisen's conscience never seemed to bother him.

Now seeing how Jaisen gets loose, London seemed to gain an ounce more of respect for'em. Jaisen's eyes were shut, he was lost in that pleasurable zone, that vibrated through his entire bottom waistline. London didn't pay the broad that was freestyling Jaisen's joint any attention.

"Jaisen." London says, his voice carried throughout the house ceasing all activities as everyone stopped and stared. Jaisen jumped as his zone was disturbed.

"Yo, let me holler at you for a minute though." London says, his timing disrupted Jaisen's mood, just what London had intended on doing. They both made their way into the bathroom.

"Yo, what happened with Breeze?" London asked, Jaisen sighed before he answered.

"We had to drop him, it was just business you know the deal." Jaisen says coldly. London smiled, from the look on Jaisen's face, London knew Jaisen felt the same way. Jaisen and London gave each other dap, then London bounced from the scene entirely.

In San Fran, Johnson was now here, with the essence of the 31st precinct behind him. From the airport, Johnson was immediately escorted to FBI headquarters, where he and Somerson would once again trade information. In most cases, I wouldn't be this important to catch, but everyone in this had an agenda.

"Johnson, it's good to see you again." Somerson smiles at Johnson's rugged request. Johnson was groggy but was at full alert when the conversation started. Somerson started his slide show.

"Crusian Ramone. One of South Americans most notorious right hand men. He was the right-hand man to this man to your left. Omant Cleosa, one of Brazil's drug lords. This Johnson, is whom was supplying the dynasty's drug supply. Crusian has set up shop here in San Francisco. Millions of dollars is flowing through this operation." Somerson says, to a bewildered Johnson.

Johnson knew I wasn't an average drug dealer, but he never fathomed such an extensive insight. Johnson was speechless.

"Berlin ran the dynasty's operation here in San Francisco. He's dead. Ron Plato, ran the dynasty's operation in Texas, now he's dead. That just leaves Crusian Ramone and Black." Somerson says, Johnson is in deep thought about what he just heard.

"So does anyone know where Black is at?" Johnson asks. Somerson gives a frustrated grunt.

"No one has seen this muthafucka in weeks." Somerson says. "It's like he moves in the shadows or some shit, but we'll get'em." Somerson says, Johnson was falling victim to the fatigue that was setting in. The two of them decided the matter could wait until tomorrow afternoon. It was at this time, I was happy that they didn't know about Leroy, in South Carolina.

*   *   *   *

Here in Jonesburgh, Traimen was just returning from his trip to San Diego. His mission was to deliver over 80 million dollars. He was to set me up an account, so when the time came I could bounce with money in my pocket.

"Shit went down?" I asked the always low key Traimen.

"No, dog, everything went smooth, the accounts set up." Traimen says in that same mellow tone.

"Black, what the hell are you doing man. This shit is wild, son." Traimen's question made me realize of how much I've kept my people in the dark. Rush was the only one who knew the entire plan. I was just hoping he could hold up his end.

"To tell you the truth Traimen, if what I'm planning doesn't work, I'm going up for damn near a century." I say to Traimen, whom had a sly smile, he now understood.

"Yo, you got any Queen cigars, I need to relax a little." Traimen continued to smile, as we made our way back to Traimen's house. In San Fran, Charlie Ave, Supreme and Majestic was checking in on Reese. The motel Reese was staying in was located near the downtown area. The sun was beaming in the always clear sky of San Fran.

Reese was just chilling letting the late night hours of partying wear off. I was hoping he was having a good time at my expense. Charlie and Majestic slowly made their way to Reese's room. Supreme was just chilling in the car, he was the lookout for unexpected visitors. Charlie and Majestic finally reach the dingy door of room 4A.

Charlie knocked three times, Reese grabbed his heat, as paranoia gripped him.

"Who is it?" Reese says, his head was throbbing still hungover from the night before.

65

"It's me, Charlie Ave. Nigga open the door." Charlie says, adding extra incentive to his voice. Reese relaxed a little, as he lowered his heat, and went to open the door. Reese never cared for Charlie, even though the two hustled for years together on Chancelor Ave, Reese always took Charlie to be a snake. Once Reese opens the door, Charlie smiles.

"What up nigga? Oh, you don't know me now." Charlie says, the sarcasm was making Reese sick. Majestic glanced around Reese's room.

"Yo, we just came to tell you in a few days we going to take you to see Black, so just be ready." Charlie says then slowly walks away. Reese shut the door not even giving Charlie Ave a second glance. For some reason the mentioning of my name rung in Reese's head. His head was hurting too much to figure out why.

Back in Manhattan, BaiRute was on his way to the Paradise. Kingsmon and Kremone was his backup. At the club Boston and Cool was in the back going over the monthly books. The bartender was doing inventory for the night supply of beverages and liquor. BaiRute and company pull up along front of the club.

The club's entrance had a red carpet leading towards the door, it made BaiRute laugh. They made their way to the front door. BaiRute's knocking caught the bartenders attention, the bartender pressed a button under the counter to alert Boston and them in back of the club. The bartender opened the door.

A chrome P-89 was flashed on him, the bartender backed up as BaiRute bogarded his way in. The bartender made a nervous lerch towards the bar, BaiRute cut'em short with a bullet in his back. With cold eyes, BaiRute watched the man slump to the ground. BaiRute pumped the man with another bullet, just for good measure.

Cool ran out with his heat blazing, Kingsmon and Kremone ducked for cover, as did BaiRute. Kremone got a good bead on

Cool's chest, with a slug to the chest he picked him clean. Sending Cool back a few feet.

Boston was trapped in the back, she cursed herself for not having a back exit. She stopped cold when she saw Kingsmon and Kremone approaching her. Kingsmon grabbed one arm and Kremone the other. Then in slow motion BaiRute eased around the corner. Fear coarsed through Boston's pupils.

BaiRute was now face to face with Boston. He smiled, then pulled a blue tip hollow point out of his pocket. He ran the bullet down Boston's cheek. Still silent, he then ran the bullet down between her ample breast. Boston squirmed, her efforts were futile as Kingsmon and Kremone grips, rivaled that of a vice grip.

BaiRute remaining silent, slid the bullet on down Boston's stomach and into her streeth pants between her legs. BaiRute slid Boston's draws over and forced the bullet into her. Boston jerked with pain. BaiRute's smile is now gone.

"Yo, tell Carlito the next one will be in him." BaiRute says, his voice colder then two day old ice. Kingsmon and Kremone let Boston go, whom crippled over in pain against the nearby wall. BaiRute and his people walked out of the paradise very nonchalant, their focus was to kill everyone in Carlito's click. BaiRute didn't know that he wouldn't haft to.

Boston waited until BaiRute and his people left. She watched them pull away, before she dared to move again. Once they were gone, Boston was making a beeline to the nearest phone, BaiRute's intimidation tactics worked perfectly. Boston was now waiting on the phone on the other end to pick up. Boston's patience was now getting short.

The line was busy, Boston was simultaneously removing the bullet that BaiRute suggestedly placed inside of her. She hung up and then sighed heavily. She dialed another number, this time the line started ringing.

"Yea, this Deon who this?" Deon says through a thick accent.

"Yo, BaiRute was just here." Boston says her voice for the first time became broken. Deon was caught off guard by this.

"What happened, I thought Jaisen got rid of him." The fuck you mean", What ever he did just pissed the muthafucka off," Boston snapped over the phone. "The nigga put a bullet up my ass, and you telling me about what Jaisen was supposed to have done. Yea, Cool, and Jimmy the bartender, they're dead. You betta handle that muthafucka!" After those words, a dial tone was all Deon heard.

Deon quickly calls Carlito this was an alarm, Deon would be damned if he would be schooled by BaiRute in the streets he fought so hard for. Avoided the Mafia and the cops to build his operation, that also expanded into the city streets of Philadelphia. Manhattan's drug game was his, and he wasn't going to give it up that easily.

Back to Manhattan, when London was searching for an outlet avenue for his pent up grief. Breeze's death opened London's head. Except he was digging a grave that to him was unknown. London knew this was all part of the game. London's mission for the time was to catch up with Sixty, whom he hasn't seen since their meeting with Deon.

London knew the temps around the crew, would remain colder then the chilliest Manhattan winter. London knew Sixty didn't care one way or the other, about the inner conflicts of the cipher. Sixty's only concern was the working of the cash flow and drug selling. London traveled with heavy speed, finally reaching his destination. Which was a gutted out building with only three floors that was sealed in.

London like the nocturnal person he is, he moved swiftly in the shadows of the building. Once London got the third floor, he saw Sixty sitting in the hallway, but Sixty was colder than usual. He was smoking a blunt, and London knows Sixty doesn't smoke.

"So what's the deal nigga, you feeling it just like I am, let's bring the snitch out dog." London says, "Or we'll be next on the hit list." London says finishing his statement. Sixty's thoughts were mad distant. He didn't haft to answer, for London to figure out that he had agreed.

Two days slid by and the air was hauntingly arid, in a still coldness. Playing the opposition to the left, a deal was about to go down. The way Ashton's been raiding Carlito's operations, Sixty isn't taking any chances. So he sent his two ladies Bracey and Keisha to make the deal. They waited patiently for the other party to arrive.

The night sky was a solid black as it seemingly crept in from a chilly evening. The other party finally arrives, Bracey and Kiesha braces themselves, both carrying heat, just in case of temper flare ups. The other party slowly makes their way over to the girls. Kiesha sized the two men up, both were husky, the bulges underneath their jackets told Kiesha that their strapped heavier.

They were now face to face.

"You two ladies have the ya yo?" One of the men asks, his voice was short and booming. Bracey raised the bag the coke was in.

"You got the money?" Kiesha says, her voice was like silk on a ruthless vibe. The two men traded looks, as if they were amused. One of the men grabbed the bag and pulled one of the ounces out. With a razor he slit the bag open. Scooping some of the coke, he then put some on his tongue, the slight vibration it caused on his taste buds convinced him of its realness.

Kiesha caught a feeling, when the two men didn't turn over the money quick enough.

"They're cops!" Kiesha yells at Bracey, the two men jumped on the girls before they could pull their heat. It was too late for the girls, they were going up. Ashton quickly runs over to assist with the arrest, as once again, he was up on one of Carlito's drug deals. The snitch was finally caught, it was time for London and Sixty to eliminate the problem.

Once down to the station, and going through the booking process. The girls got their one phone call. Kiesha dialed a calm seven digits. The phone rang a few times before the other end picked up.

"Yo, this Sixty, what's the deal?" Sixty says calmly.

"Yo, we got set up, they talking about sending us up for a good sixty." Sixty realized that Kiesha was calm but she was scared as hell. Sixty with no response, slowly put down the phone hanging up on a confused Kiesha. Whom was shocked when she heard the dial tone. Sixty called London whom was chilling at the moment with Boston.

"Yo, my nigga what's up?" London says, then takes a sip of his sour whiskey.

"You were right, I know who the fucking snitch is. We about to mope this nigga out baby." Sixty says in one long breath. A sign to London that Sixty was excited. The hunt was over, what was left was to kill the prey.

* * * *

Back here in Jonesburgh, Traimen and Rush were cruising in Traimen's beamer, on their way to Brown's house. She was Traimen's former running partner, she was going to help us with Crusian. Traimen drove slowly through his old neighborhood streets, letting the people soak up his success with envious eyes.

A black caddie pulled in behind Traimen and Rush. Traimen drove relaxed, not noticing the stealthy black caddie in the back of them. The occupants of the caddie were cocking their automatic weapons, and was ready to take aim. The caddie pulls alongside of Traimen and with a simultaneous reaction, bullets started flying from the caddie.

Traimen and Rush quickly ducked for cover, with no time to grab their heat, death was almost a promise. Just as quick as the shooting started, it abruptly stopped. Rush slid out of the passenger side door and began to walk up the street. Traimen with his body heavily soaked in blood, lay slumped in the drivers seat faintly breathing.

Rush pulled his cellular and dialed 911, then he dialed the cab company. Rush caught a cab back here to Traimen's crib. I was stunned to see Rush so calm after such an incident. It was clear to me now that Crusian wanted to flush me out of Jonesburgh. At that moment I didn't know why, but I was soon to find out.

"Damn, I'm telling you Black, those were Crusian's men." Rush says, his voice reflecting his calmness. "Why doesn't he just come and get it on with?" Rush says, his tone echoing in frustration. I had to ease his mind and at that mine too.

"See if he snitches on us, everyone will label him a snitch, so he can't afford to rat." By my own words I had an apeline, Crusian couldn't rat us out, so why not flush us out to the police. I couldn't figure out why, the reasoning of this, at this point, Johnson was the furtherest person from my mind. My cell phone started ringing. I picked it up in the middle of the second chirp.

"Yea." I answered without saying my name, to be cautious of a phone trace.

"Yo, Black this Leroy baby. Check out this fire, my nigga." I sighed in relief, hearing Leroy's voice reminded me of the tranquilness of South Carolina's atmosphere. "Yo, they got the feds on this one son, I heard Johnson from Westgate was on his way out there. He's got some kind of special consultant status on the case. Those muthafuckas want you bad Black, but I got your back though."

Leroy's southern accent carried his words in long drug out syllables. For Leroy to be down south he had mad connections. I was glad to have him on my side.

"Damn, how the fuck they figure I was in San Fran, is beyond me Leroy. Yo, keep your people steady on my club in Atlanta. I'll handle the shit out here. Son, how's Brandy holding it down." I asked, trying to feel out his opinions of her.

"Shit dog, my people's feeling that broad my nigga, she's crazy sweet. But yo, handle your business, hold that shit down like Shamon would've hold ya head. Peace." Leroy says then hangs up. Leroy this one nigga has been there since the beginning and obviously to the end. I glanced at Rush whom was calmly pulling on a backwood, I knew I had to move fast.

My plan was coming around in full circle, but it was coming too quick. My hypothesis was that drug bust that involved Perry somehow brought Johnson here. Things were getting deep and I had to follow that same adysil road. A few hours later, me and my people moved to a hotel here in Jonesburgh. It was just my paranoia, in this situation it was a good ally.

Rush was outside, he was on his cell phone with Crusian once again, plotting more extensively on my soon to be untimely demise.

"Yo, that shit went smooth. Traimen's in the hospital now with his chest caved in." Rush says to Crusian whom is smiling to himself on the other end.

"So what's Black's next move? I need to know these things Rush. I want Black to be dead by the end of all of this." Crusian says, his voice carried unconsciously through its tone. Crusian has just made his intent clear, for what his relationship with Rush was all about.

"Yea, I'll see if I can't make that happen for you, Crusian." Rush says then beeps out. Rush's mind was running a hundred miles a minute, the situation for him was starting to flex on his mind. Rush regained his composure and made his way up some winding steps, that lead to his room.

Back over at Traimen's place, the police was there and so was the feds. Once the feds found out about Traimen's connections with me, Somerson and Johnson lept into action. They were there quickly, hoping to catch me slipping.

"Damn, I thought he would be here." Johnson says, his voice highly agitated in tone.

"Fuck, he knew if Traimen was in the hospital information would get out, so he moved his entire operation once more." Somerson says, his mind racing with possible locals for me to set up shop again.

"Wherever he's at now, we'd better track'em down quick and get this shit over with." Johnson says to an agreeing Somerson. Johnson on the inside was burnt, he's dealt with me before but knowing what he knows about me now. Changes the rules of engagement. He now has to adjust to my ways of thinking, those same ways Shamon so diligently taught me.

Back in Manhattan, Carlito's click was thinning out, BaiRute was coming on strong. A relentless attack it seemed BaiRute was posed on killing everyone in the crew. Carlito's thoughts went to the memory of his other brother Quick, whom was killed by Shamon after a botched hit in Brooklyn.

Carlito knew that Deon was well on his way to seeing an early grave. It was time, Carlito thought, to get out while he could still breathe. Every breath Carlito took could be seen in a swirling mist, his mind laced in the promise of the future. Time was flowing counterclockwise, it played against Carlito's life span.

Carlito needed to relax, the crew's street value was shaky. Ashton and myself was pressing them to death, literally. Carlito knew why BaiRute was here, he was my way of taking over New York. Carlito shook his head in disbelief for not seeing BaiRute coming. Carlito's thoughts were disturbed by his cell phone ringing. As the phone rung, he found himself dreading to answer it.

"Yo, what da deal?" Carlito answers, his voice groggy from exhaustion.

"Yo, this Deon baby. We got hit by BaiRute again. Luckily this time no one was killed." Deon says, the whole time Deon was talking, Carlito's mind was funneling over their current situation.

"So where's he at now, is he holding up in Manhattan, and where's Jaisen?" Carlito asks, now slightly agitated, Deon smiled, knowing that Carlito is sharpest once provoked.

"We'll know soon enough where he's holding up. Jaisen is holding it down with Boston at the Paradise.

"Awright, meet me down there." Carlito says then beeps out. The night was creeping on below zero temps, a chill wrapped around Carlito's neck as his cable was laced in exotic fashioned ice. As Carlito drove his cherry red coated gold datened Benz down to the Paradise. His weary but stable mind was traveling a path of its own. That silencing thought of leaving the team flashed from one temple to the other.

When Carlito pulled up to the Paradise, his mind became a freezing ground. He just didn't feel right. Carlito shook his head and walked on into the Paradise. Carlito glanced over to the bar with a cold, but sentimental glare. the club didn't feel right, Jimmy wasn't there to hold down the bar which he did in a respectable fashion. Also, missing was Cool, Carlito never imagined that he'd miss the coolness that Cool presented.

Carlito slowly made his way towards the back, he seemed to move with a ghostly presence. Once to the back, Carlito was greeted by a smiling Boston.

"My nigga, where you been I haven't seen you in days." Boston says, her eyes sparkled as she smiled within them. Carlito half heartedly smiled back at Boston.

"yea, where's Deon, he was supposed to meet me here." Carlito asks Boston, whom just hunched her shoulders and offered no further response. Carlito's attention then became diligently focused on Jaisen whom was enjoying a Philly black, ignoring irrelevant conversement, that would disturb his comfort zone.

"Yo, Jaisen, what's up my nigga? Dog, the word on the street is, we hanging with BaiRute, but he's still getting in our ass. What's the deal son, you need more people, more guns, what?" Carlito says to a seemingly unattentive Jaisen, whom

74

was thoroughly relaxed, letting the tension of current events float away with the smoke that vacated his nostrils.

"I got BaiRute covered, you just handle the business end. I'm going to hold my own, you cool with that." Jaisen says, his last reply was a question that Carlito wasn't going to dignify with an answer. Carlito knew Jaisen was going to get his man. James wasn't going to be dead in vain.

"Yo." A voice range out, everyone looked towards the door. Deon has finally made his appearance. In his face, a tired almost complacent look was apparent.

"What's the deal son? I'm here, and you late." Carlito says, jokingly with his older sibling. Deon smiled a little at his younger brother, before he spoke again.

"Check this out my niggas, Ashton is pressing my block peoples. So don't tell no one about drops or pick ups, we're gonna haft to start doing that shit ourselves." Deon says, although he seemed in control, quietly on the inside, he was hemorrhaging with panic. Carlito knew from Deon's last words that their street value was just about vanquished.

Carlito couldn't believe this shit was happening, he was for the first time, in a long time, feeling the confusion and haste of being desperate. He had to do something, anything. All the sudden, leaving became his second option.

* * * *

Now that London and Sixty knew who the snitch was, it was all a matter of time before they would push his wig back. London was once again on the solo, in his car leaving Brooklyn's Redhook, pushing sixty. London received a page from one of his runners, London knew where to meet him and was on his way.

Once there to meet his runner, London noticed no on was in sight. London sat for a moment, weary from being caught off guard. London decided to parlay in the car for a second.

London's eyes drifts to the cut, near the street entrance. London noticed a figure emerging, very quietly from the shadows.

London took heed to the runners entrance, it was a little mysterious for him. London slowly steps out of the car, where he was greeted by Manhattan cold. This effected London very little, as underneath his coat his burner stood fast with heat.

"Yo, what's the deal son? What's the problem?" London asks. The runner didn't reply quickly enough for London. Smelling something foul, London reached for his heat. London with his vision to a minimum due to the street lights pale glow. He failed to see the four-five the runner was holding.

London was snatched and throwed back, by the sheer force of the bullet that hit him, once the runner let the gun burst. London fell to the ground violently. The runner with no remorse, slowly walked up on London's now hollow body. The bullet completely took out London's chest cavity. Two men run up from behind the runner.

"Yo, Deon what you want done with the body?" One of them asks, as all three men stare down coldly at London's frail body.

"Dump his punkass in Redhook, and make it look drug related." Deon says then slowly walks off. Now all was next is Sixty. Meanwhile, in upstate New York, near Albany, James and Jaisen was checking up on one of their contacts. This particular contact hasn't been in touch for more than four days, this wasn't normal for people who dealt with Deon on a business level.

James pulled to a stop in front of the contact's house. They cased the place before they got out of the range. The snow made a crackling sound as the two stepped on the snow. They finally made it to the front porch, where a repugnant smell stopped them cold. James and Jaisen noticed how the door was forced open, as it laid slanted on the bruised hinges. James and Jaisen drew their heat, and eased very slowly inside the door. The sight they saw caused the brothers stomachs to turn. Their contact was sitting up right on his couch with a slit that went from his chest to his stomach.

"Damn, the fuck was he doing. He must've been fucking with some Jamaicans." Jaisen says, to a smiling and nonsurprised James.

"Yo, I'm going outside to get some air. This shit is fucking foul, yo." James says then turns to walk to the front door. Once outside the brothers inhaled the fresh air. James cell phone was a welcomed distraction.

"Yo, this James who dis?" James says as he and Jaisen was on their way back to their range.

"This Monty, ya'll better come see this." Monty says his southern accent tainted, it was slowly crossing over to its northern counterpart.

"The fuck is you talking about nigga?" James says, his patients short from the sight he just witnessed.

"I just found London's body here in Redhook. I'll see ya'll when you get here." Monty says then beeps out.

"What the fuck is wrong with you?" Jaisen asks a mystified looking James, whom didn't give Jaisen's question an answer. James just shook his head in disbelief as they finally pull off in the range.

Two hours later, Redhook was bathing in an open silence. James and Jaisen was slowly walking towards London's slain body. The two stared at the body before they spoke, Monty glanced at the two brothers dumbfounded facial expressions.

"What the fuck happened to him?" Jaisen asks Monty, whom informed them of London's dead body, shrugged his shoulders.

"Dunno, but he's one dead nigga." The country Monty says through a winey voice. James and Jaisen left London's body where it lay.

Henry Vereen IV

Part IV

Henry Vereen IV

Black Whispers

While sipping on my dark elixir, my mind was flooded with the thoughts of, how is my plan going to end up. New York was only a few steps away from being mine if BaiRute flips this time, its over for him. Playing the background was uneasing but easy to pull off. At this time, the most imperative thing was to keep Somerson and Johnson away from Traimen.

I knew Traimen wouldn't talk, but to make sure of his silence I sent Supreme and Majestic to be his personal muzzle. In the Crawford district is where the hospital was located. Traimen was exiting the hospitals front entrance. Supreme and majestic was there waiting for him, Traimen slides into the backseat of the mirror tinted renta car.

"Yo, what's up my niggas, ya'll chilling right." Traimen says, trying to feel out Supreme and Majestic's interior motives. The ride was quiet as Supreme pulled to a stop down by the beach. Traimen shook his head as he knew he was about to die. Supreme turned just enough as he then pushed his snubbed nose into Traimen's face. One shot was let off.

Supreme and Majestic was now dragging the body out of the car and onto the beach, where they left the body. It was meant to look sloppy, to throw the police off my trail. Supreme and Majestic pulled off slowly. Traimen's death was an unfortunate casualty of the game.

Rush was now in my room, pacing back n forth, with growing aggravation, Rush paced harder. I took a sip of dark and then a pull off of my Queen cigar.

"The fuck are we waiting for." Rush suddenly says. Something was eating at this Red negro, I just didn't know what at the moment though. This ancyness was spreading through my people, they weren't used to just sitting still.

"We're waiting for the right moment to move. We've got to let them move first, just a little while longer. Shits going to fall where it should." I said to Rush in a stern but cold tone. It was just enough for the moment, to cool that blaze running through Rush's body.

Damn I thought this shit really is complicated. How Shamon pulled all those games off, on Tolip and Johnson back in the day. Was something, damn I wish I could call on that nigga, pull out my head some of his thoughts, but that's awright though. I got to move swift with mine, this is my time to shit.

*   *   *   *

Back in Manhattan, unaware of London's death, Sixty carried on the clicks business like time was his allie. Sixty was preparing the drugs to be moved that night, Carlito personally relayed that message to him. In the three story lab, sat two freezers. One was used for drying out Sativa leaves, left with the seeds to strengthen the potency of the flavor.

The second freezer sat adjacent to Sixty's position. This freezer contained the finish product, Black Velvet. This was Sixty's recipe for one of the hottest products on the streets of New York. The weed consisted of: chronic, chocolate tide, and coke with a touch of wet wood to solidify all of the ingredients.

The coke and wet wood is what made the product addictable. The wet wood caused the weed to burn slow, as the coke will severely jazz you up. Sixty in his own rights was a remarkable chef of Sativa blends. Time was moving with the process, Sixty nodded to himself approvingly.

Outside of the gutted building, like rats scurrying about, Ashton and his people were creeping. Ashton and his crew moved quietly up the building's steps, and quickly gained their necessary positioning. Ashton took a brief moment to assess the situation, he checked his heat and gave the order to move in.

Guns were ablaze, but Ashton had the element of surprise. Ashton put a bullet in Sixty's chest and the rest of Sixty's men received the same fate. In ten minutes, Ashton's people bagged the drugs and then abruptly left. Ashton looked at Sixty's slain body and a venting smile crossed his grill, he then slowly turns and walks out.

"Yea." Deon says, as he anxiously awaits the report on Ashton's last raid.

"Yea, this is Ashton its done Deon, we'll see the money soon son, no doubt about that." Ashton says then hangs up. On the other end, Deon sat with a crooked smirk on his face, smiling, thinking about the money.

*   *   *   *

Manhattan was icily heated as Carlito drove, his destination a backstreet near Spring Street, where he is to meet BaiRute and try an diffuse the situation. Carlito was pressed with desperation, his mind now a trap for negative thoughts. Those thoughts would haft to wait because BaiRute at the moment was not mentally right.

Pulling to a stop on the backstreet, Carlito noticed BaiRute standing in front of his Benz waiting for him. Beside BaiRute stood his cousin Carlos, who's hand was on his heat in case of a set up. As Carlito approached BaiRute, he secretly cursed me for sending this nigger. Once close enough the two eyed each other, with contempt.

"What the fuck you call me out here for nigga." BaiRute says, while never loosing eye contact with Carlito. Carlito's facial expression showed no emotion.

"I thought we could talk money, and end this long discussion, that we've been having with our guns." Carlito says, he paused to see out BaiRute's reaction.

"I'm willing to cut you in on some of the profit. But I'm going to need a few days to get the money." Carlito finishes then awaits a reply. BaiRute thought to himself for a minute.

"I'm feeling you on that, yea I'm feeling that. You got three days. Yo, if you're fucking with me dog." BaiRute says then smiles, no more had to be said, as Carlito caught the future meanings of BaiRute's words. Now the meeting was over, with one problem temporarily solved. The other problem could be handled.

Over at the Paradise, Boston was awaiting Deon and Carlito to arrive. The club was starting to get busy, the new bartender looked apprehensive as he shuffled elixirs back and forth. The people danced to up to date music, as the dance floor was full of moving bodies. Boston was suddenly taken back when she saw Jaisen, he wasn't usually there during business hours.

Boston's curiosity quickly peaked, as she made her way over to meet Jaisen by the bar. When Jaisen noticed Boston he smiled.

"What's the deal shortie?" Jaisen says, his words were crystal sharp as Boston seamed to be in awe.

"Nigga, I should be asking you that. Is Deon and Carlito with you?" Boston asked, seemingly trying to give herself an excuse for Jaisen's present.

"Na, I'm rolling for self tonight. I'm just going to chill." Jaisen says, his voice was eerily relaxed. Boston just couldn't figure out why he was there. Boston quickly decided to leave the situation alone. She then walked off, glancing back at Jaisen, a chill caressed her thoughts.

Over at the entrance of the club, Deon was making his grand appearance. Deon not being a fan of suites, was deferring to a jean suit and boots. The cable he wore, rubies and ice, fashioned into a mariners cross, the cross itself was pure ruby as the chain was linked diamonds. The only thing missing was Kia on his arm.

At the bar sipping on whiskey and rocks was Jaisen, watching the flossing Deon. His thoughts were heated right along with the whiskey he was drinking. Jaisen at this point decided it was time for his departure, he really didn't want to talk to Deon. He had always held a disdain feeling for the man.

Jaisen wanted to leave, before the whiskey made him act on this feeling.

Jaisen knew he would soon see Deon again, but not on friendly terms, that he was sure of. Jaisen avoiding Deon as he maneuvered through the club. He made his way out the entrance. He jumped in his ride and headed out to Redhook, looking for a good fight or crap game, whichever one, it didn't matter to Jaisen.

Carlito's thoughts were smoky as he drove, the conversation he just recently held with BaiRute was his main focal point. Although it went well, Carlito still could hear, that voice of desperation whispering in this ear. It held a ghostly essence, sparking vivid visuals like a prophet in a trance. Carlito knew now what he had to do, he needed to speak with Ashton.

Coming to a slow stop, Carlito looked over towards the Paradise, which now to him looked like a C-class dive. He parked his car down the street, and slowly walked back up to the club's entrance. At the door, Carlito ran into the usual groupies, and bystanders. Carlito was getting tired of the same ol scene.

Once inside the club, Carlito went straight to Boston's office, where an all iced out Deon sat.

"Damn son, you look stressed, what's the deal baby?" Deon says to his younger brother, whom didn't smile at Deon's subsequent remark.

"Yo, I need a dime or something, I got a headache like a muthafucka. Yo, Deon where's Ash-?" Carlito says as he caught himself. Deon looked at Carlito in a curious manner. Carlito smiled. "Damn son, you like fluorescent tonight aren't you?" Carlito says changing the flow of the conversation. Deon smiled with a flare of arrogance. Carlito smiled also, but his thoughts still remained on getting at Ashton.

Back here in Jonesburgh, Somerson and Johnson were on the beach standing over Traimen's dead body. They took one more cold and long look before the body bag was zipped up.

"Damn, this was too sloppily done to be a hit by Black." Somerson says to Johnson, whom was in disbelief.

"This could be a set up to throw us off." Johnson says., while stroking his mustache inquisitively.

"I don't think he's that fucking shrewd." Somerson says, seemingly dismissing the idea, but on the inside Somerson was enjoying the challenge. To him this was like a bloody chess game, except every move now was crucial.

"Son, I've been a cop for many years, and I've learned and still is learning shit is not always what they seem. Especially with Black." Johnson says, in these last few days, Johnson was developing a plan to catch me, but he's just decided to share it with Somerson.

"I don't think Black's left the area, run checks on local hotels from here to San Fran, and all surrounding areas within fifty miles. It's time to start thinking like him." Johnson says to Somerson, whom smiles as he thinks his investment, in Johnson, is finally going to pay some dividens.

Back here at the hotel, Brown, Traimen's former running partner, was making her way up the winding steps, that led to the second floor. Rush and Charlie Ave, were outside smoking cigars. Rush's eye was caught by Brown. She moved slow with gliding steps, her eyes were a dark brown, they glistened when the sun played in them.

Brown stopped as Rush approached her. Brown eyed Rush, in a cautious way. She then glanced at Charlie Ave whom was fondling his heat.

"I'm here to see Black." Brown says, her voice wasn't waverly as she came across direct.

"Who's Black?" Rush says, his eyes cold and unreadable.

"The one Traimen was hiding, so if you're not him, I suggest you take me to the muthafucka." Brown says calmly, her temper reflected her style, relaxed but treacherous. Hearing all the commotion, I stepped out into the walkway. Brown's eyes lit up. I looked her up and down, she was crafted like a fine sculpture.

She was a pleasant sight, as she walked by Rush she cut'em a cold side glance. From that Rush smiled. Now Brown was directly in front of me.

"I'm sorry about Traimen. Any word on his condition?" I asked, Brown's smile became a distorted frown.

"He's dead, they found him on the beach this morning." Brown says, as for a moment she gathered herself. If she only knew that I'd had him killed, maybe then her coming here would've been more eventful. I invited her into my room where Mojo and Korlane sat at a little table drinking some beverage.

"So how'd you find me?" I asked, it was a cue to Mojo and Korlane. The wrong answer and I was going to cancel our conversation.

"Traimen told me where you would go if shit got hot. He was thorough like that." Brown says. The way her response came, I knew it was truthful. I could see why Traimen ran with Brown, she was an above average broad. She reminded me of Brandy, when she wasn't thinking with her ass.

"So why are you here? Traimen's dead, what's your angle?" I asked, Brown's eyes dropped to the floor as if it held her response.

"Let's just say working with you is my closure." Brown retorts, her direct gaze which was now directed towards me, was that same look Traimen would give me if something went over his head. I offered Brown a drink, she refused.

"I like to keep a clear head." She stated, I was starting to feel weary of this broad, but I knew somehow that she would be useful.

Back in Manhattan, BaiRute like a true general were addressing his troops.

"Yo, fuck that money, and fuck Carlito, and Ashton. We about to take Manhattan baby." BaiRute says, as he had intentions of renigging on his previous deal with Carlito.

"We got to find those muthafuckas first." Carlos says, trying not to laugh, not in amusement but at the fact there was going to be more violence.

"I know where they're at, so get you're guns ready." BaiRute says unknowingly about to step into an unchartered range of his thinking.

The next night, Carlito was strangely staring at his chrome, his thoughts settled on Ashton, he put his Benz into gear and pulled off onto Spring Street. The rain was at a steady pace as the evening hours slowly eased in Carlito's intentions were cold, his mind now eclipsed of any righteous thoughts, desperation has finally won out.

Carlito was on his way to meet Ashton, this would be the first time he's ever met Ashton. Carlito couldn't wait for the face to face confrontation, he was going to execute an agreement, rather it be by money or death. Carlito knew on the inside something had to give, but he knows Ashton's the only one that is going to get it.

While Carlito drove, he was tightly being tailed by BaiRute. BaiRute was with Kingsmon, that's all he would need to get the job done. BaiRute knew something was wrong, because he knew Carlito was a loner but not during most evening hours.

"Yo, why don't we just do this nigga, he's solo, so lets just drop'em." Kingsmon says as he cocks his piece. BaiRute smiled to himself.

"I got this feeling he's going to let us kill a few niggas with just one bullet." BaiRute says then looks at Kingsmon. "Just be patient, all those niggas will soon be out." BaiRute says, with enough tension behind his words to make his point to Kingsmon. Twenty-five minutes later, Carlito pulled to a stop, over in the train yard. BaiRute followed along with Kingsmon silently. Carlito quickly made his way to the meeting spot.

Ashton stood impatiently as he watched Carlito approach his position. Ashton tossed the cigarette he was smoking to the ground. Carlito stopped on the dime, as now a stare down commenced.

"Carlos, what brought you here from Philly?" Ashton says coldly. Carlito smiled, noticing how Ashton used his real name, in mockery.

"Yea, I wanna settle this, bring in some cash, and take out the bullets." Carlito says, his smile now a plain scowl. Ashton's brow was now in a frown, as he felt an uncertain vibe from Carlito.

"You sound like BaiRute, he offered chips as well. What makes your offer special?" Ashton says, his words, stirred an array of emotions.

"With my offer, you ain't got no choice." Carlito says, then pulls his heat, Carlito then threw the money at Ashton's feet. Ashton knew it was the devil or the presidents. Either way Ashton knew hell would be his closure. Ashton looked down at the money, then back at an icy Carlito. Ashton wasn't moving fast enough for Carlito. Carlito put two bullets a piece in both of Ashton's knees.

Ashton, with a loud scream, buckled to the ground. Carlito then steps up and puts the gun to Ashton's head. Ashton smiled then started talking.

"You stupid fucka, when you're through with me, put a bullet in Deon as well." Ashton says grinning. "Yea, that's who your fucking snitch is. James, cool and Jimmy and other members of your crew died because of him. All the raids and arrests, who the fuck you think informed me. Only Deon could've done that." Ashton says, Carlito now peeved, put one round in Ashton's dome, leaving him sprawled out on the gravel ground of the train yard.

BaiRute couldn't believe what he'd heard, he waited until Carlito pulled off in his car before he moved. BaiRute had a smirk on his face. Kingsmon the same.

"Like I said my nigga, one bullet for a couple of niggas." BaiRute says to Kingsmon.

"I'm feeling that baby. I'm going to chill for a minute." Kingsmon says, with a sick smile. As he could see the green lining his pockets. The two was now sitting in the Benz. BaiRute was dialing my cell number.

"Yea, this Black, what's the deal?" I said, as in my left hand my dark elixir was on ice.

"Yo, this BaiRute baby. New York is ours, ya know in a couple of hours anyway though." BaiRute says, I didn't detect anything indecent about his voice.

"So what happened?" I asked, knowing that BaiRute would give me a very brief summary.

"Lets just say your boy got popped, I'm out." BaiRute says then beeps out. On my end I took a sip of my dark and then an unconscious grin slowly spreaded across my face.

*   *   *   *

In San Fran, Crusian was screaming on his right hand man, Juan. He was scorning him about loosing track of my progress. Juan was cool though, used to Crusian's venting sessions, it bothered Juan very little.

"We've got to bring some light on him. He seems to be a step ahead of those fucking cops." Crusian paused for a flecting moment. He then looked at Juan with a smile. "Go to this hotel and shed some light on our situation." Crusian says his voice held an edge that riveld anti-freeze. Juan reached out for the paper, took it and eased quickly out of Crusian's office.

Here at the hotel, the sun was beaming, and with no breeze it was really ablaze. I was out in the parking lot, talking to Korlane, about my next course of actions.

"Yo, check this, go to the Grand Doscine and make arrangements for the crew. You've only got one hour, so be quick baby." I said to Korlane, whom at the moment looked distant in thought.

"What about that bitch," Korlane says, then pauses thinking up her name. "Brown." He says, in his words you could hear his distrust in her.

"What of her?" I aksed, sincerely amused at Korlane's concern. Korlane looked at me with his brow in a frown.

"Dog, I smell a wet rat baby, something ain't right about that broad yo." Korlane says, then walks off purposely not giving me the chance to respond. For the first time, this cold silent snakish nigga whom was infinently cool in any situation left a bug in my ear. With my cane in hand, I made my way back up the winding stairs and back to my room.

Everyone was already getting their stuff ready. The reason I was moving again, was to keep these negros sharp. I didn't know at the time, that some of Crusian's men were on their way here. But my team stayed strapped and alert. Rush was the only one not phased by the unrelenting heat, that seem to liquify all my body. This damn place reminded me of Mexico.

Hermasillo, where I almost lost my leg in a shootout over drug money, with then drug lord Demarco Seze. Yea, but that's a whole nother volume. For a moment things went silent, then guns started singing to sixteen bars. Mojo was front line with Rush, Charlie Ave, Majestic and Supreme for his help. Crusian's men were shooting at ghosts, as Mojo and them moved around like speical ops.

The shootout lasted for a short two minutes. I shook my head in amazement, all that shooting and no one got hit. Around the hotel you could see the occupants faces pressed against their windows looking wide-eyed at us. At this moment, a single thought gripped my mind. We've been made. It was a play to put some heat on us. Damn I thought we're going to haft to vacate qiuck, as cops would be swarming soon.

We got to our cars quick and drove out the back parking lot exit. Ignoring the speed bumps we almost flipped over them, going at reckless speeds. Coming through the front of the hotel's parking lot, the police were coming like a swarm of bees.

I shook my head, as I heard those sirens singing those poinsenous notes, of jail time.

Crusian's face was pictorially floating around in my mind. He must think he's dealing with a street virgin, with no experience. It was on now, it was time to ice the heat with cautious pursuit. An hour later, we were just checking into our new hotel. Korlane was there when we got there, oddly enough so was Brown.

"Yo, Rush, let me hollar at you for a minute." I told Rush as I pulled him to the side, as everyone else was on their way to their rooms.

"Yea." Rush says, his voice calm and collective. It seems the just happenings effected him little.

"Yo, I want you to play Brown close, see what that bitch really wants." I told Rush, Rush nodded his head understanding as he then walks off. Brown was now suspect, she shows up, then the fives, she had my third eye wide oepn. I wasn't going to switch hotels anymore, this would be my last place of stands. The next time I swtich locals it'll be countries.

As I settled down, now in my room, my Queens cigar was in full blaze. The scent of the smoke alone had me feeling the contact of the situation. I opted to chill alone, as I knew the dynasty was going through a strong metamorphic phase. BaiRute was going to take over New York of course, though, one of my boys would be there, to make Rush's pressence felt. It was changing but all for the better.

Back at the hotel we vacated, Somerson and Johnson were starting to get close.

"Damn, we almost had'em, just a few minutes earlier." Somerson says. Johnson shrugs his houlders in a frustrated way of motion.

"There's something here that Black wants, but what, I can't put a finger on it. If he wanted Crusian dead he would've tried already to kill'em." Johnson says as he and Somerson traded perplexed looks.

"Maybe he wants San Fran?" Somerson says to Johnson, in an atempt to pick Johnson's mind. Johnson met Somerson's question with silence as a theory started to evolve in his head.

"He wants something but, San Frans a little too funny for Black's style. The business is a little to fruity for him." Johnson says, then walks back to the car. Somerson laughs as he felt they were getting closer. The two were now on their way to San Fran's 16th precinct on the westside. They were playing the angle of Traimen's involvement with me.

They were going to find out about Traimen's partner Brown. If they found out about her, my plans for Brown would be severly dampered. That damned Johnson, was finally using that razor sharp intelligence that made him one of Westgats finest detectives. Too bad he started to use it so late.

*   *   *   *

Crossing the Brooklyn Bridge, Carlito was on his way to Redhook, a place he hasn't been to in years. Carlito now knew that leaving Manhattan, New York wasn't an option anymore, it definitely had to happen. He knew he would go solo back to Philly as he ws going to leave Boston in Manhattan to run the Paradise.

Carlito's mind was clear, as he drove he knew what the deal had to be. To make up for: London, Sixty, James, Cool, Simmy, plus the bullet that was shoved up Boston's ass. He knew the consequnces of telling Jaisen, and was well beyond comprehension, prepared to accept them.

Once off the bridge, Redhook was only seconds away. Carlito's only been to Jaisens spot once, and that wasn't a very welcomeing experience for him, as he and Jaisen drew heat on one another. Carlito was sick from the inside out. The way things seemed to, in a short second, start to plumet. Carlito was now in front of Jaisen's place.

93

The rain that fell like vapor, covered Carlito's car with a fine moisture. Carlito stepped out his car, people on the street mostly the hustlers, watched with hungry eyes. Carlito paid the poeple inside the building's lobby no heed as he traded cold looks with them. In the far corner of the lobby was a crap shoooting Jaisen.

Carlito walked up on the game, he first noticed the pot was full of c-notes. Then Jaisen threw the dice, the dice counted up eight. They used the usual two green and one red dice combination. The game seemed to stop when one of the participant noticed Carlito standing with them. On that note Jaisen recognized Carlito and pulled up from the game.

"What the fuck, nigga, you lost or something right?" Jaisen says, his voice scratchy, but raspy due to the effects of hte nighttrain he was drinking.

"Yo, step outside with me though, let me hollar at you a second dog." Carlito's expressionless face, eased Jaisen's mind, that this, Carlito coming out there wasn't no bullshit. The two made it to the doorway, then finaly outside. The rain now was coming down lite and steady, with an abstract rhythm as it tapped across the concrete.

"What's the deal son, you out here, something must be wrong my nigga." Jaisen says to a non smiling Carlito.

"You still looking for BaiRute?" Carlito asks, he paused awaiting an answer.

"Yea, but I can't find where he's holding up at." Jaisen says with spite in his voice.

"Well, Deon's the reason why your brother and your operation is dead. So forget about BaiRute and handle the real reason. I'm out." Carlito says then begins to walk off.

"Yo," Jaisen began to say something, but decided to let it go. It just danwed on him that Carlito was giving up on his own brother. Jaisen shook his head, then walked back inside of his building. Carlito pulled off, now headed back to Philadelphia. Jaisen was now involved in a one sided conversation, Bell and

Nathan was down for whatever. Jaisen has no more respect for Deon, so his life meant little at this point.

Over at Deon's place, he was on the phone with an excited Boston.

"Yo, they found Ashton's body, laid out on the gravel and shit. He was in the train yard." Boston says, happy for what seemed like a lucky break for the crew.

"Forreal, they know who did it?" Deon says, not showing his frustration.

"No, they say it looked like a deal gone bad, or some shit. I'm saying though that's one less muthafucka sweating us." Boston says, Deon was silent for a moment.

"Awright Boston, I'll hollar at you tonight at the club." Deon says then hangs up. Deon's mind was racing, as he couldn't figure out who murdered Ashton. Deon realized that he hadn't seen Carlito since that last night at the club. That thought faded quick, as Deon couldn't believe Carlito could know about his dealings with Ashton.

Deon sighed heavily, as his thoughts were fleating as they came across quick, with blinding speed. A figure in the living room doorway caught Deon's attntion. Kia stood there with a concerned look on her face. She didn't like the look on Deon's face, which was one of surprise, and a tinge of frustration. The two traded glances, Deon's eyes drop to the floor.

Kia shook her head, in a very calm disgusted way. She walked away from the living room entrance, once again leaving Deon to his own miserable thoughts. In a brief thought Deon wanted to reach out to Kia, but his stubborn pride restrained his voice. Deon was now stuck, nowhere to turn, voided at his own interpersonal crossroads.

Now rolling through the streets of Manhattan, was Jaisen and his boys. The respect, that little once of respect that Jaisen once held is gone. Deon was now a minute nigga to Jaisen. In the backseat, Bell was loading the pistols, riding shotgun was a quiet Nathan. They were just pulling onto Prince Street, when a lite snow started to fall. Bell handed Nathan and Jaisen their guns from the backseat.

They all checked their heat, and with their eyes as black as cole, and hearts heavier than souless assassins. They were ready for their hit. Jaisen pulled to a stop in front of Deon's flat. All three of them jumped out the car, with their straps in hand, they wlaked up the stoop's steps.

Jaisen nocked on the door three times, then rang the bell. Kia slowly made her way to the door. She looked through the peephole, seeing it was Jaisen she deeply sighed in dissapointment. Kia slowly opened the door. Jaisen quickly slapped Kia with his burner. She stumbled back into the wall. Bell and Nathan quickly steps in.

Deon hearing the ruckus, made his way to the doors area. He stopped in his motions, when Jaisen pointed the gun at him.

"What the fuck is wrong with you nigga?!" Deon says, hearing the fright in Deon's voice, made Jaisen smile. As Jaisen was squeezing the trigga, he had James picture in his mind. The gun bursted with anguish aiming the bullets. The bullets struck Deon high in the sholder, as Deon fell he saw Bell and Nathan drag Kia into the living room by her hair.

Jaisen walked up on Deon, his eyes a feverish cold look. Jaisen waited a couple of seconds, just so Deon could hear Kia's cries for help, as she was unconsentingly being penetrated by two men. Deons heart was racing, he jumped when Kia let out her loudest scream, yet. Jaisen's smile was now militently suggestive.

Jaisen pulled the trigga and let hateful bullets caress Deon's cranium. Jaisen, without a second glance at Deon made his way into the living room. Bell was now thorugh as he then switched with Nathan. Kia lay on the floor balled up in obvious pain. While Nathan was doing his thing, Jaisen walked away and on out the front door.

Bell cocked his piece, Nathan was on top of Kia shivering as he let loose inside of her. Nathan took his time getting up. He zipped up his pants, and then smiled at Kia.

"Damn you got good pussy." Nathan says as he's walking towards the living room exit. Bell pointed his heat at Kia and shot her four times, permanently ending her pain. Bell was the last one to get into the car, as Jaisen then pulled off.

In all the shit I've seen, heard of in the past year, this by far was the grimiest shit. yea, but that's just a Redhook nigga for you.

*   *   *   *

San Fran for the first time, was cloudy and cool, for it to be winter, a straight week of sun seemed to be the norm. Rush was now on the solo, he was on his way to meet Crusian. Rush was sort of ancy, feeling uneasily amped by this so called meeting. He knew something wasn't right, but Rush knew how to play his cards.

Rush pulled to a stop in front of a cigar shop. Which was located at the bottom of the hill that made up the street. Rush looked thorugh both corners of his eyes, before he entered the shop. Once in the shop, the cashier looked at Rush, over some low cut reading glasses, peculiarly.

"Yo, son," Rush says, then glances at the Titans next to the cash register, "let me have a couple of Cubans." Rush says to the man as he stared the man in his light brown eyes.

"Let me show you to the back, sir. We just got some in." The man says, his voice barely above a whisper. As the man quickly made his way towards his back space, Rush quickly fell in step. The man stopped and pointed Rush to an entrance that led into a secluded hallway. The hallway had three round lights that hung from the ceiling, they swayed to the breeze created by the a.c. blowing through the vents.

At the end of the hallway, there was a brightly lit room, with a lone talbe in the middle of it. Around the table sat Crusian and two of his boys, whom smiled at Rush, when he came into the bright room.

Rush peeped out his surroundings before he took a seat at the table. The two, Rush and Crusian traded cold glares before the converstaion.

"Wath's the deal Crusian? Why you trying to put a leash around my neck?!" Rush says, feeling uneasy. Rush's facial expression was cold. Crusian smiled.

"Why isn't Black dead yet?" Crusian asked, his voice perplexed due ot the situation.

"Now is not the time," Rush says then pauses for a moment. "It's too early we do it now everything looks fucked up." Rush says to a now peeved Crusian.

"I tell you when its time muthafucka and I say now is the time." Crusian says as he stared at Rush with flames in his eyes.

"Man fuck you, I'm the one that has to do it, take it or fuck you!" Rush says, then calms down before he starts to speak again. "Yea, Browns finally in the picture. You should've brought that bitch in earlier." Rush says, to a now calmer Crusian.

"I tell you," Crusian says, with a crude smerk.

"When Blacks dead, business between us will be beautiful." Crusian says, then gets up from the table, and with no more words walked out the room. Rush sat at the table for a few minutes to let Crusian and his people get a head start.

Once back on the street, Rush was examining his situtaion. Was it going to be my plan, or his way to Rush the answer was easy so he figured to carry on the way he felt he should.

Back here at the Grand Docsine, I was entertaining a phone call from BaiRute. He was unusually excited, as for the current events in Manhattan, I probably would be to.

"Yo, these niggas are killing each other out here and shit." BaiRuite says, his cloudy accent came from his rare excitedness.

"What happened?" I asked, seeing if I could picture, what he was about to tell me.

"Black, Jaisen killed Deon, and yea Carlito murdered Ashton, like straight smoked that muthafucka, you know what I'm saying?" BaiRuite says into the phone. A smile crossed my face. New York was now mine.

"Any loose ends? If there is sowe them up and hollar at me later." I told BaiRute as I then hung up the phone. I took a sip of my dark elixar. A nock at the door, deceased my brief moment of silence. As I turned towards the door, Brown was standing there.

She wore a red miniskirt, her legs were thick and brown slightly shimmering with the glare of baby oil. The touch of six inches caused her ass to sit stout. Her hair hung low around her shoulders, some of it covering her left eye.

In all, she looked like a hooker on Yamen Street, on the Island. I smiled as she stepped, as her breast bounced in rhythm with each step she took. I put my glass down heeding the warning of this siren. Once again a poisonous note was being played, even at this sharp angle I couldn't resist this opportunity to nock it down.

*   *   *   *

Manhattan seemed to be still in the moment, due to the effects of current situations, it would be quiet for a long time to come. The weather was icy, a far cry from the comfortable temps out here in San Fran. Kingsmon and Kremone were sitting outside their Benz smoking their unusual blend of herb they sat and waited.

The Paradise was jumping still, so Kingsmon and Kremone had a long wait ahead, but by then they would be blunted beyond comprehension. the night went by slowly as early morning hours crept up with snail speed. Finally, Boston walks out the

Paradise's side exit. Boston didn't notice the Benz parked outside. Kingsmon and Kremone smiled at one another.

Boston made it to her car, right when she got in, Kingsmon and Krmeone was right up on her.

They were bluntedly precise in their swiftness in movement. They were on both sides of the car. boston was breathing heavy upset at herself for not being alert enough. The first time she was ever caught slipping would be her last.

The two fired their guns until both of their guns were empty, making it an excessive but thorough hit. The two walked back to their Benz with a slow pace. They were too blunted to notice the white Lexus pulling up. The two got to their Benz and then drove off to where BaiRute was holding up.

Through the driver side window, of the white Lexus, Jaisen looked at Boston's bullet riddled car. He shook his head in disgust. In his thoughts Boston deserved a better fate then that. Jaisen decided to follow Kingsmon and Kremone. Then he would brake for his own stride, and finally let James rest.

As the rain picked up, on the inside of BaiRuites hold up spot. BaiRute and Carlos stood in the window talking.

"Yo, I need you to go back to the Island and be my gneral there." BaiRute says to his cousin with a patient smile. Carlos didn't return his smile.

"What the fuck, go back to the Island, what the hell am I goin to do on the Island." Carlos says, his tone causing BaiRute to take a second look at his cousin.

"Damn dog, you go to the Island, you can make that shit hot again, the fuck nigga, once I start running this shit here in Manhattan. Nigga you could be set for life." BaiRute says, Carlos gave BaiRute a tired look as he gathered his thoughts. A sudden nock on the door, relieved some of the pressure that was buidling up between the two cousins.

BaiRuite slowly eased over to the door, with his piece in hand, he looked out the peephole. He saw a quiet Kingsmon and

Kremone. He opened the door slowly, and then slowly walked off. Kingsmon and Kremone casually slide inside the door.

"Is it done?" BaiRute asks, his voice hung in the air, as Kingsmon began to speak.

"Yea, but Jaisen wasn't there." Kingsmon says, as he takes a seat next to Carlos on the champagne colored leather couch. BaiRute shook his head.

"Damn, that's awright though I got a feeling we gonna see that nigga soon, yo." BaiRute says, then turns his attention back to his cousin.

"You going back to the Island, in the morning so get your shit right." BaiRute says, this time his tone wasn't so patient.

"Yea, whatever nigga." Carlos says, in his own way ending the conversation.

Outside of BaiRutes hold up, Jaisen's white Lexus pulls to a stop. Jaisen was on the solo, as after the situation with Deon, he dropped Cool and Nathan back off in Redhook. Jaisen cocked his 380 and grabbed his wind barrel nine. Teflon down, jaisen was ready.

This wasn't business, it was exotically personal. Jaisen would feel resentment if he didn't do this. The rain was starting to thin out. Jaisen exited his Lexus and began to coldly stroll towards BaiRutes apartment building. Once on the inside, Jaisen took the back stairwell. In this stairwell, he saw pissy smelling bums, prostitutes that occupied their business spots.

With a cold glare, Jaisen walked by these people with a cool breeze. Jaisen had the drop on an unsuspecting BaiRute. Jaisen finally made it to BaiRute's door. He looked down both sides of the hallway. Then with his 380 he nocked on BaiRute's door. The nock caused BaiRute and his people alarm. Everyone in BaiRute's click was present, so nines were now being cocked.

Jaisen was outside the door listening to the guns being cocked on the inside. Jaisen stepped back, and let his 380 go. The door rocked off of its hinges in a maming face. Jaisen stepped through the now doorless entrance. With his guns blazing, Jaisen's eyes were wide with enthusiasm, this was his style, his flair for the dramatic.

BaiRute and his people were srambling and ducking the last of his people to try and hide was Carlos. Jaisen with vengeful aim, caught Carlos in the chest with a few bullets, sending Carlos across the floor with a trail of blood. BaiRute noticed how his cousin was sprawled out in the floor, laying in a pool of his own blood.

Everything went silent in that instance, as BaiRute's P-89 seemed to gleam in a sinister light. BaiRute rose up from his hiding place. His sharpened aim by his new hatred for Jaisen a single bullet dropped Jaisen. BaiRute quickly walked up on Jaisen. He gripped his steal tighter as a sudden spurt of rage went through him, BaiRute bit down on his bottom lip.

He unloaded the rest of the clip into Jaisen's now holey body. BaiRute glanced over at Carlos, whom had Kingsmon and Kremone looking down over Carlos's dead body. BaiRute turned coldly facing what used to be a door.

"Yo, we can't stay here, we gotta get the fuck out of here." BaiRute says to his crew. BaiRute walked out the apartment without giving Carlos or Jaisen a second look. Kingsmon, Kremone, Ramone and Lu-wayne followed BaiRutes instructions silently as they all slowly walk out the apartment.

An hour later, BaiRute was in front of a payphone. Once BaiRute got my number and his card right, he stepped into the booth. He picked up the receiver and dialed my number. As he waited on me to pick up, he stared into the beads that formed on the booths glass by the misty rain that had been falling all night. BaiRute's breathing was faint, as around him, he felt the air of grief thickening around him.

I picked up the phone on the second ring.

"Yo, this Black who dis?" I said on the other end I could hear raspy breathing.

"Yo, this BaiRute, you know those loose ends you were talking about. They've all been sowed up." BaiRute says in his voice I could here pain.

"You awright! You sound winded my nigga." I asked seeing if he would tell me. On his end there was a brief pause.

"Dog, I got to be moving my nigga." BaiRute says, his voice was mildly distant.

"Yo, BaiRute," I said, my voice was serious and low. "How does it feel, now being a real general?" The response to my question, was the dial tone in my ear. For all the people I knew and know in this game, BaiRute was the only nigga left in it with his soul intact.

Henry Vereen IV

Part V

Henry Vereen IV

Pearl Rum

In San Fran, Johnson and Somerson were becoming the new dynamic duo. They were braking my case down slow with a through ease. The last hotel we were in, is where Johnson and Somerson, began the final leg of their investigation. Somerson was starting to feel ancy, knowing I could drop dime on him at any moment. Feeling that dirty uneasing heat, he had to come up with something quick.

"Damn, this kid is hard to catch." Somerson says, his direct tone amused Johnson. How the hell did this kid become an Agent, he's a fucking bum, he doesn't know the field for shit. Johnson thought.

"Yea, he's hard to catch, but this is a little out of Black's element." Johnson says, then pauses to gather his thoguths.

"Somerson, have your people check the local four star hotels for recent check ins under the name of West., It's a hunch, but I bet he's somewhere under our noses. He doesn't have anyone else out here to hold up with. In due time son he'll show the fuck up." Johnson for the first time took a page out of Shamons notebook, it was about time he started thinking like we would've.

Somerson kept his cool, his feelings of contempt for me was steadily growing as were those same feelings growing for Johnson, too. Somerson chose to perp on the left, for its complexity and mystique. Hiding behind the feds was a perfect mask for his merky, shadowy in the flow talents. Somerson didn't want me alive no more then Crusian. Death was the only way to liquify his problem.

Johnson was frustrated that he couldn't move solo through San Fran, he didn't know this city like he knew Westgate. Somerson was too slow for Johnson's mental pace. Johnson wanted me arrested quick, or on the sly make me disappear.

107

Johnson and Somerson were now on their way to the 13th precinct.

Somerson new the leutinent, they had information on my people's shoot out, something to give him an excuse to come after me with full force. Once the two reached the leutinent's office, they were both quiet lost in their own penetrated thoguhts.

The leutinent was all smiles, as he greeted Johnson and Sommerson.

"Well fellas, let's get to it. We have reason to believe that the men shooting at Black's people were Crusian's people." The leutinent says. Johnson's mind completely stopped on that thought. Why would Crusian's people be trying to kill Black. Johnson quietly thought, that one threw him for a loop. He thought that Crusian and myself would be friends instead of foes.

"I'm telling you fellas now, in a few moments we're going to have a war on our hands. I know of one party. I need your info on the ohter, more along the lines of what they're capable of. And how do we stop this from happening." The leutinent says, sincerely asking for help. Johnson felt compelled, he felt the leutinent's plight.

He knew shit culd get ugly, if I flipped it wasn't meant for milquetoast personalities to be involved.

"We need to find out where he's hiding. And as you just suggested its urgent." Johnson cut to the quick.

"That's where we're stuck, its so many possibilities, but Johnson thinks he's holding up in a hotel." Somerson adds as his two-cents worth.

"Alright, I'll put some of my best people on it, but let's put a fucking fire under our feet." The leutinant says, staying arridly cool throughout the conversation. Johnson and Somerson left the 13th precinct, a step closer to apprehending me. The two rode silently back to San Frans F.B.I. headquarters.

Johnson was loosing his mental composure, the patience required for the hunt, was slowly easing away. The gripping thrill, the suttle but raw intensity, that ran rampid on his soul. Johnson was eager but weary for the first time he was close. Somerson felt similar, except his goal, was to simply silence the scapegoat.

*   *   *   *

The heat not only moved thorugh the atmosphere, it moved with intentions to burn me. Between the heat, my usual dark elixar and most recently Brown's tirless sex, my head was spinning. San Fran was starting to get dark, the whole scent of this sunny city was starting to become stale. I wanted out, but that was impossible.

I'd rather kill Crusian instead, but that would come at the right time. My Queen cigar was still, halfway smoked and resting in the ashtray. I haven't seen Rush for almost a day now. Hopefully he's playing his part of the plan. His part was crucial, the main link of my course of actions.

Korlane stepped into my room unannounced, with a sly grin on his face, I knew he had something good to tell me.

"Yo, you got your ticket?" I asked Korlane, with no smile on my face. He took heed to my seriousness.

"Yea, I'll be in New York by Thursday night." Korlane says, in his voice I could hear his excitement. He's always wanted a Major peice of the pie, but I've always kept him close, schooling his mind for this.

"When you get there, your first piece of business is to resolidify Deon's connects with us. Don't change nothing, just let shit flow as it's been. Just let them know they're going to be dealing with you and BaiRute now. Manhattan's finicky and no side hussels with the mafia, or cops. We don't want to end up like Deon or Ashton." I told an intensley listening Korlane. Korlane was now ready to go. New York was his, and I know

Korlane would run it right. Once again my indirect approach to this game worked. Korlane stood up from the chair he was sitting in, he gave me dap, and with a slick bop walked out the door. I slipped back into my thougths once again.

Korlane like Rush was my prodigy, I put them in this game. I kept them both close, and half fed. That kept them, from being able to fuck me over in the long run. Damn I was placing seeds all over the map, Rush would soon be in charge of San Fran. Korlane got New York, and I got Brandy in the Southeast.

Brandy and Leroy, damn. I know Leroy won't let her go astray if anything, with her his business would go even smoother. When Brandy wasn't thinking with her sex tools, she was a formible mind to come up against.

Over on the otherside of the Grand Doscine in the lobby area, Rush and Brown were discussing their plans.

"So when do I get to smoke Crusian's ass." Brown asks, her rage stimulated by Rush telling her it was Crusian's people who killed Traimen.

"We haft to wait and see. The police and feds are on us. They got shit hot for miles. It won't take long before they find us." Brown looked at Rush her slanting eyes were telling of her frustration.

"Fuck all that! I just want to put a bullet in that muthafucka." Ignoring Brown's comment Rush was in deep thought.

"Yo, check this shortie," Rush suddenly blurts out, "We haft to bring Crusaian out, to even the odds a little." Before Rush could say anything else, a slight vibration in his left pants pocket gained his limited attention.

"This Rush, who dis?" His words snapped with spite, due to his short patience.

"It's me."

"Waddup son?" Rush says, his words now a lot calmer. He was wondering what I wanted at this particular time.

"Yo, I want you to set up another meeting with Crusian, this will be my last time talking to him." I told Rush whom went silent for a moment.

"Heat?" Rush asked in a curious tone.

"No doubt." I told'em then beeped out. I could picture the smile Rush had on his face. He grabbed Brown and headed for the lobby's exit.

In the cab on his way to the airport, Korlane was contemplating his next situation in New York. He couldn't help but wonder how this prism of selected schemes would paly themsevles out. He thought about the past events leading up to this. The burning down of Shay's Point, before that his main partner Dukane senslessly being murdered.

Korlane wanted to disappear but this was all he knew all that he could grasp onto. Korlane wasn't a gun holder, he was a money getter. The type that should've been on Wall Street instead of Chancelor Avenue's cold corners, shooting dice, and hustling. It's funny how life's cards are dealt.

You got asses with millions, and geniuosues with nickels, it's a damn shame, Korlane thougtht. I'm twnety-four years old, and ain't got a damn thing to show for it. Look what this slick shit done brought ya, fast money, fast women, expensive whips. Danm would I trade this shit for a good woman, a family and a house in the suburbs.

Korlane laughed at that thought. Causing the cab driver to give him a woundrous look in his rearview.

"Fuck no!!" Exploded in Korlane's mind making him laugh even harder. All this shit I've been through and ain't got caught yet. I need to just chill and let the money come to me. Korlane thought his laughter became a slight smile. Yea, let those big face muthafuckas come to me.

Korlane smiled as they turned onto the exit leading to the S.F.O. airport. He was looking forward to running New York, even though his third eye had to be oepn constnalty for a sneaky

BaiRute. Nevertheless, Korlane has found his nitch in life. He was a hustler, a Westgate thoroughbred with a lot of sense.

The evening was slowly creeping in, as Somerson was through playing agent for the day. After drooping Johnson off at his hotel; Somerson was on his way to a San Fran suburb named Rose Meadows. He was on his way to meet the laying low Crusian. As Somerson drove through the Meadows, he was amazed at its beauty.

The way the houses seem to gleam in the moonlight, the way Roses played in every other yard. Red Roses were the most abundantly sighted, but in Crusians yard White Roses filled his entire front lawn. Somerson pulled into the driveway slowly, and then stopped. Crusian himself, was outside to greet Somerson. Somerson braced himself for the face to face meeting.

"Somerson, long time no see, ah." Crusian says in his phoniest sincerity. Somerson gave Crusian a crude smile.

"Crusian, I have bad news." Somerson says then scopes out the scene for any unknown hit men." The police have a finger pointed at you, they think you're at war with Black."

"And if I am?" Crusian asks Somerson, his words laced with bitter sarcasm.

"The police want you and Black, so what's the deal Crusian?" Somerson asks, a now non-perplexed Crusian.

"So give them Black. You've got connections, so use them, let them know of the situations at hand". Crusians says, with a smile on his face.

"Damn Crusian, if Black's a problem you must be loosing your touch." Somerson says, leaving Crusian to his thoughts.

Crusian with a distant gaze watched Somerson drive out of his driveway. Crusian wanted me dead with a pure passion. In those type of thoughts, it wasn't a nice feeling to have myself as the main focus.

A few chirps of Crusians cellular phone, brought Crusian's focus back around.

"Yea," Crusian says, his accent vibrated with patience.

"This Rush yo, Black wants another meeting. I think he's finally coming around."

"And you don't know if that's it?" Crusian asks, Rush wanted to hang up, but he smiled the urge off. Rush knew I was playing on Crusian's nerves.

"What time dog?" Rush asks, hurrying the conversation along.

"Two o'clock, tomorrow afternoon." Crusian says then beeps out. Crusian didn't know what to expect, so in being a vet at this game he prepared for the worst. Crusians thoughts of me, were comparisons of hisself when he became Omant Cleasas right-hand. The way I moved, was similar to his tactics. Except my doe, wasn't long enough to buy a whole fucking police force.

Crusian shook his head with an admiring smile, not of envy, but of being reminiscent of his own brash youth. Both of us came up militantly decent, quiet and icily bred. Crusian slowly made his way back into his suburban castle. The front lawn's lights went out, Crusian was through for the night.

Moving with a silent speed, Black's queen cigar smoked slowly. In his thoughts he felt Johnson's essence, that familiar presence. Black knew this was the final stretch, it all rode on his seemingly forever changing plans. Charlie Ave drove tensely through San Fran illuminating streets. They were on their way to see Reese.

In a two car caravan, Black's people were on the move like heated Nomads. Rush wasn't present, as he stayed behind to watch out for Black's other vehicles. Black for the first time, was out in the streets. Black's eyes, were chinky from the effects of a long tote of his cigar. Charlie Ave pulled to a stop in front of Reese's hotel.

Mojo whom was riding shotgun, was the first out of Black's car. then Charlie Ave . . . In the other car Surpreme and Majestic exited their vehicle. All four met for a brief moment.

Then they began to ascend towards room 4-A. They were there within seconds. Charlie knocked on the door three hard times.

Surpreme and Majestic, pulled out two empty thirty-eights. Reese groggily opened the door, before he could recognize whom was at the door. Surpreme hit him with the butt of the thirty-eight, then Majestic opened up on him with his thirty-eight, Charlie Ave, and Mojo stood by and watched the thorough beating.

"Bring that nigga on, we ain't got all night!" Mojo says. Surpreme and Majestic picked up the blood soaked Reese. Once they got down stairs, Surpreme and Majestic put Reese in the trunk of their car. Black watched silently from the back seat of his car. Black just took a long pull off his cigar. Charlie and Mojo made their way back to Black's car quickly.

The two cars left just as quickly as they came. A slight pace of rain, took Black back to his thuggish days, back in Westgate. When hell is wet, Black was the best secret kept. It was hot and Black would be the equator, Black knew it was time to take his stand, and let his plans more aggressive tendencies show. From Johnson to Crusian, Black was erotically sober, his mind as sharp as a jagged blade.

Back at the hotel Rush was talking with Dutch, one of Crusian's men. The lobby was full of people, mostly just arriving tourists.

"Go handle your business, its the gray Geo. A level five of the parking garage." Rush whispers in Dutch's ear.

"Yea, Crusian will be pleased, I'll let him know how cooperative you were". Dutch says. His mile, a devilish cheese grin.

"Word, I'll let'em know how your fat ass needs to lose weight." Rush says with no smile. Dutch's smile evaporated.

"What! Watch your mouth." Dutch says his voice a dead calm.

"The gray Geo muthafucka." Rush says then - walks off. Dutch hated Rush with a passion, but in Rush's way of thinking, they can take whatever he's saying any way they wanted. He bit his tongue for no one, not Black, not Crusian and most definitely not for a lackey like Dutch.

Rush watched Dutch walk off, Rush deviated to play the lobby as he awaited Brown to return from Jonesburgh. On that thought, Rush's pager exploded in his pants. Rush looked at his pager, seeing an unfamiliar number caused alert. Rush debated on even calling the number back.

He couldn't afford not to. So he pulled out his cell phone. He slowly dialed the number back. The other end rung twice. With his nerves frozen with uncertain suspense, Rush waited in an agitated state.

"Rush?" A voice on the other end suddenly blurts.

"Who the fuck is this?" Rush says, his voice boomed over the phone.

"This Brown, they got me here at the police station, they got feds here."

"What the fuck you there for." Rush retorts his voice still fiery with impatience.

"They want to know about Traimen and shit." Brown explains, her usual sharp tone, was now panicky and borderline sparadic. Rush's inner calm now rises to the surface.

"You don't know shit baby. They can't arrest you on the truth ya feel me. Tell them what you know." Rush tells a now silent Brown. Brown was dumb-founded, she knew nothing so what was Rush getting at.

"But I don't know shit about what happened." Brown sounded flustered by the whole situation.

"Exactly. You don't know shit, so how can you help them. Just be cool, and repeat you don't know nothing. Call me when they let you go" Rush says then beeps out, leaving Brown comfortable and somewhat confident of herself. Rush looks over towards the entrance of the lobby, where he sees a lone standing Mojo waving him down.

Rush in a nonchalant manner, made his way over to Mojo's location. Mojo looked sort of calm, but Rush knew him too well to ever think that.

"Where's Black?" Rush's voice was low and sharp.

"He's back in his room with our other guest." Mojo says slowly. Rush caught his emphasis on guest.

"Did anyone see ya'll moving the body." Rush whispers, Mojo shook his head, no.

"Where's Brown?" Mojo asks, now noticing Brown's absence.

"They arrested her in Jonesburgh, some shit about Trainman's passing". Rush relays to a now thinking Mojo.

"What if she plans to rat?" Mojo asks in general curiosity. Rush sighed, hoping that wasn't the situation.

"She knows not to talk, and if she does , she's dead." Rush says ending the conversation. The two made their way up to Black's room. Rush had to see Black about Brown.

Brown was panicking, her inner voice was soothing her feelings and doubt. Brown's been in this situation before. She didn't understand why she was so disturbed. Yea, she was tight with Traiman, but no love was involved in their relations, Brown's thoughts paused once she saw Somerson and Johnson walk into the room.

Somerson and Johnson stood and acessed Brown before they spoke to her. Brown kept an ice grill never showing her uneasiness.

"I'm Agent Somerson and this is Detective Johnson. Somerson was trying to cause a false relaxation to take place. Brown didn't know them personally, so she didn't give a fuck what their names were. Johnson was taking in Brown's dark brown skin complexion. He took in her lean but thick body, her legs and jet Black hair. Johnson wasn't lusting for her, but comparing her to Black's past companions.

116

"Let's get right to it. We know about your involvement with Traiman, and Traiman's involvement with Black." Somerson says, leaving the tact to Johnson to figure out.

"Brown." Johnson says then takes a seat across the table from her. Brown was turned at Johnson's accent. It was a dead give away, that he was from Westgate. To Brown, Johnson sounded a lot like Black, except a little harsher in tone. "We know you know where Black's holding up at. So just tell us, and you can walk out of here. Or would you rather have a lawyer present?" Johnson looked coldly at Brown, whom seamed unfazed by either Somerson or Johnson.

"I don't know nothing." Brown says calmly, Johnson's mind momentarily went back to Perry's code of silence. What does Black do to these people to gain such loyalty. Johnson shook his head. Such a beautiful woman, she wasn't guilty, and Johnson believed her when she said she knew nothing.

"Do you know how much time you could get." Somerson snaps. "Now! One more time, where's Black?"

"I told you I don't know nothing!" Brown yells.

"What hotel are they holding up in?" Somerson screams at Brown. Brown with a cold stare glared at Somerson as the two locked eyes.

"I don't know nothing." Brown mouthed, her voice now a dead calm. Johnson looked at Somerson, then motioned for them to step outside, they walked outside.

"Somerson looked evilly back at Brown, whom looked at him, her eyes still and cold. Somerson shut the door behind them.

"Somerson, she doesn't know anything, not nothing she can help us with anyway." Johnson tells a now heavy thinking Somerson.

"So lets set her loose, and see where she takes us." Somerson says, then walks off. Johnson couldn't figure out what was really bothering the ecstatic Somerson. He figured there was more at stake than Somerson led onto. Johnson went into the room and told Brown she could go. Johnson watched Brown walk away, to Johnson she was just another youth throwing her life away.

The next morning, the sun was submerged behind thick clouds. Slowly as sunrays started to break through, the fog was burned off. In front of Brown's place in Jonesburgh, sitting in a blue Taurus was Somerson and Johnson. They had followed her there the night before. Hoping she would unconsciously lead them to Black.

The two of them sat in silence. Johnson once again was thinking of Somerson's actions the night before. What the hell is it, that this fucker isn't telling me. If I didn't know any better, I'd say he was a crooked son of a bitch. But like they say, all's done in the dark, will soon come to the light. Johnson's thoughts froze, as Brown suddenly emerges out of her front door.

Somerson was also, jolted out of his mental hiatus, as Brown now in her car, made it down 3rd Street. Johnson was at a safe distance to tail her. She wasn't going to evade these two determined law enforcers. As they followed Brown, they were giddily excited, as wondering where she was going, made them anxious.

Brown made a stop four blocks away from the Grand Doscines. Brown continued on looking to her meeting up spot. Brown was surprised, when she saw Surpreme instead of Rush. Rush figured the feds would tail 'er, so why not send someone they're not familiar with. Brown was nervous, not because of meeting someone she hardly knew.

Only because "she wanted out of the entire situation. The pressure was slowly beating her down. She wanted to kill whomever did Traimen, feeling as though that would alleviate her burden. Brown was now easing over to Surpreme's positioning. Surpreme cut Brown a full smile, as to insinuate he was pleased to see her.

Brown didn't buy the smile, she knew a live wire when she saw one. With this cat, she had to watch her tongue, it was crucial, for her conversation to go smooth. Brown didn't want to become a victim. Surpreme's smile left his grill, as he noticed, Brown didn't return the rare, but friendly gesture.

"Damn shortie you look vexed." Surpreme expressed, although he didn't care, he had to ask, just to let her know he noticed.

"Ya'll niggas are in some shit, them cops are thinking that ya'll killed Traimen. I think ya'll need to lay low for real'. Brown gives Surpreme a look that carefully conveyed her words.

This bitch thinks too much. Surpreme thought. "Damn baby, the way you talking, it sounds like you done sold us out." Surpreme says, then smiles that same deceitful smile. Brown stepped back she prepared herself for the unknown.

"Why didn't Rush meet me?" Brown asks, playing <u>nieve</u> to the obvious.

"The fuck you mean, why he didn't, because them fools was going to follow you." Surpreme retorts, his patience now borderline or none. "Stop asking so many fucking questions and listen." Brown's ears stand attentive. "Go home and chill, we'll call you, so don't do shit suspicious alright" Surpreme says then turns and starts to walk back to his car.

Brown stood there stunned and frustrated. She knew she was lucky it was broad daylight. Brown returned to her car and sat for a moment, letting her mind regain it's composure. Across the street, Somerson and Johnson was peeved at such an acute dead end.

"Damn, I forgot Black's' father was a cop, he would anticipate us following her." Johnson says to a smiling Somerson. The two decided to follow through with tailing Brown, whom has now pulled back onto the street. Somerson's cell phone started ringing. Somerson picked it up after it's second ring.

'Yes," Somerson says into his phone.

"Yea Somerson we've got something on the case, and its good I'll tell, when I see you." The dial tone was quickly heard.

I think they got what we're looking for." Somerson says to a slow driving Johnson, whom just smiled.

The sun was in a brilliant blaze, with it's sunrays showering the ground at gentle speeds. Black and his crew was now leaving the Grand Doscines. The lobby was crowded, but the crowd took heed to the cold looks on their faces. The crowd parted as Black and his people flowed by with an icy presence.

Black and Rush trailed behind the rest of their crew.

"Everyone's heated dog, how you going out." Rush asks trying to see where his mental should be set. Black thought about Rush's question.

"Nigga, shits just like Chancelor Avenue, just a little deeper." Black counters.

"So shits starting to get wet?" Rush asks, as a sharp delight sped through his heart.

"For sure my nigga, when we get there, keep your heat about you, like on the dime and shit." Black relays calmly.

"I think Crusian will chill, he wouldn't want to bring heat to this spot." Black agreed to Rush's comment.

"shit, that muddafucker probably snorts that candy. So don't think, he won't blaze on us. Keep your eyes open." Black says. Rush decided to let the conversation drop; Rush noticed how Black took his attitude to another level. This was the side of Black he'd heard about, but never witnessed. Rush knew he was in for a treat.

Once they were outside, they both paused when Surpreme pulled up. Black couldn't help but smile. He enjoyed having live units in his click, it proved to be helpful and hazardous at the same time. Surpreme quickly jumped in the car with Majestic. Finally the crew was on their way to Crusians suburban hide away.

Black was escaping into his thoughts, in these last few days, Black would haff to let his abstract soul show. The one, he felt

120

the bitter sequel. The soul he would have to escape to, he didn't want to, but that feverish accent of adrenaline was slowly taking him back. The violent temperament mixed with is arctic intelligence, made up Black's acute disposition.

The ride to crusians spot was tension filled and paralyzing. The two rent-a-cars were in a sequential order. In the first car and heated was Charlie Ave, Majestic, and Surpreme. While only seconds behind, was Black, Mojo and Rush. Finally the two cars pulled into Rose Meadows. The crew noticed how immense the houses were. But Black was too caught up in his thoughts to be impressed.

The two cars stopped in front of a house, that had a fresh Bently parked in the driveway. Black and his people flowed out of the cars, and up to Crusian door within seconds, Mojo knocked twice. The door slowly came open, a small lady stood in the doorway, her gray uniform was set off with a white silk apron.

She stood off to the side, as Black and his people made their way in. Off to the side of the hallway sat the living room. It was furnished in all white leather accompanied by crystal ends and coffee tables reflecting with an ample effect bounced sunrays of many colors around the room like a huge prism.

The extensive hallway lead into a pool room; where a marble pool table sat, on the table pearl made balls were spread across it. Black and his people, on the cue of the servant lady, took a seat each on one of many stools. A few moments went by, and then suddenly, Crusian and his boys with frowning faces walked calmly into the room.

Crusian's cool eyes set on Black, then he peers at Black's people, whom sat ready for anything that could possibly happen.

"Black," Crusian says through a snakish smirk on his face. "How are you doing?" Crusian finishes his question, his eyes still colder than hail. Black's eyes were affixed on Crusians eyes, in them Crusian could almost count his last few days.

"What's this deal, Crusian, you flexing?" Black's tone made Crusian think twice about his response.

"Flexing. On you, no I didn't do nothing of the sort. Look, Black, I recently found out that the feds and cops want us. Why would I bring heat on us like that. We're no pushing dimes, and nickels and shit. This here is nothing but Ya Yo, the purest of all kind. We've got the best shit on the market from here to New York, or in your case Westgate." Crusian explains, Rush glances at Black.

Rush knew Crusian was bullshitting, playing both sides was tricky, do you pull your gun and blow the session, or let this fall as it may. Damn, one fucked up move and this shit turns shittier. This is a fucked up situation, this shit is making me ancy. Just chill nigga, be cool. Rush thought to himself as he continued to listen to Black and Crusian egoes go at it.

"What's to stop you from dropping dime on us muthafucker?" Black's icy exterior infuriated an already aggravated Crusian.

"You come into my house with this shit? What would stop me from fucking you, right here?" Crusian yells. On this note guns were drawn with clips fully loaded ready to release their hollow holdings. Black and Crusian glared with contempt at one another, each one not tolerating disrespect in no manner.

"You, think I'm bullshitting. This isn't about pushing weight." Black says, he stands off his stool, with his cane in hand, he decided to show himself the way out. Everyone slowly put their guns away. Crusian was steadily seething with rage. He watched Black and his entourage leave his pool room.. Crusian's people all looked surprised, Crusian secretly admired Black's guts. But Crusian had other things in mind for Black.

Even though catching Black has been an tedious, process Johnson and Somerson were now right on Black's heels.

"This is it. See, All the Hyatts, Sheratons and etc. All have thousands of check ins, every six or so months" Roberson says to an ancy Somerson and Johnson.

"What's the point Roberson?" Johnson asks. Somerson concurred with a strong silence.

"The point is they wouldn't hide there, it would be too obvious. So I checked out the B-List of four star hotels. The Grand Doscines, the Cape of the Bay, the Oscar view Palace." Roberson continues.

"Damn Roberson! Have you found 'em yet?" Somerson booms and showing his short patience.

"Yes I have, someone checked in under the name Drake Black at the Grand Doscine, with three adjoining rooms." Roberson finishes his statement.

"So he could have a couple of family members with him." Johnson relays, feeling as though Roberson ran into another dead end.

"Check the date and time. October sixteenth, five PM, two hours after that shootout at the Motel 8". Roberson smiled, seeing the expressions on Johnson and Somerson's faces. Roberson seemed to enjoy the facing of success.

"Yea, we finally got that muthafucker." Somerson says, in his chest, he let an exhilarated sigh loose. Johnson reared back in his chair. He shook his head in relief.

"Damn, now we haft to come up with away to get at Black without causing a shootout." Johnson's tone was barely above a whisper. Somerson, caught up in the stress relieving moment, didn't give that a thought.

"Yea, maybe we might haft to wait him out. Or drive him out." Somerson's last comment brought a smile to Johnson's face.

"Man Black's too cool to be smoked out. We'll haft to wait 'em out. And besides we really don't know yet if Drake Black is a real person or one of Blacks aliases." Johnson calmly conveyed to his counterpart. Roberson's smile got wider.

"Johnson, Somerson" Roberson says, "Drake Black doesn't exist." Somerson liked how this information was flowing.

Johnson was finally starting to feel better, remembering his promise for closure he was driven.

"Let's see if Brown can tell us something now. "Somerson suggests to an agreeing Johnson. The two, with the help of Roberson was finally on a roll. They couldn't miss with this information. With this situation normal procedure wouldn't work. Johnson knew Black's father, he figured the man taught Black how to avoid cops and Feds. Johnson knows Black is no easy target for simple shit.

The two now on their way to Jonesburgh, was submerged in case closing thoughts; but that string of doubt still lingered in their minds. In Johnson's mind, the thought of finally bringing in Black, played around. Although they now had something, that would bust this case wide open. Johnson was betting on this next talk with Brown.

Johnson knew once they talked to Brown, she'll get in contact with Black. Then her life would be in danger, cause Black had a pet peeve with lose ends. Johnson knew they had to play this card right. He wanted Black, but not bad enough to get people killed to do it. But Brown already knew the consequences, in her case she would just be a sad casualty.

Somerson, could finally silence his scapegoat, if word got out, about him and Ron Plato's connection. His career would be over. Plus Crusian was also in business with him. His life was the true definition of being in limbo. Black seemed to be that thin line he stood on, one loss of balance, could cause him to see the opposite side of life. Crusian was now his biggest threat to his career.

Exit 21 to Jonesburgh, this sign meant a lot to this Agent and Detective at this moment. The faster they get to her, the more they felt like a burden, was being lifted of their shoulders. Minutes later, Johnson pulled to a stop in front of Brown's place. They took a deep breath, and with sheer confidence flowing, they made their way to Brown's front door.

Somerson knocked twice, those hard knocks caused Brown an uneasy feeling. She went to the door quickly. She peeped throughout he peephole. Brown's mind went into a frenzy. I did what I was told, and here they are again, Brown thought. She quickly gathered her thoughts and opened the door. Her cold glare, had no effect on either Johnson or Somerson.

"Why ya'll harassing me?" Brown says coolly. Johnson gave Somerson a quick look, Somerson knew to let Johnson handle the conversation. Johnson didn't need Somerson's ampted up behavior.

"Brown, things are serious, and we know about your connection with Black." The pause in Brown's response; told Johnson, she was ready to dime out, just a little bit more pressure. "Can we come in?" Johnson asks, his voice never leaving its still water calm.

"No! and why do ya'll keep telling me about this cat Black or whatever his name is?" Brown retorts. Johnson knew he'd had her flustered.

"Look, Black doesn't care about you; that should be evident in how he smoked Traiman." The way Brown's eyes dropped to the ground, Johnson knew he struck a nerve. Damn girl, just give' em up. Johnson thought. Somerson stood by amazed at Johnson cool and patient manner. He was finding out what made Johnson one of Westgate's best.

"We found out that Black had Traiman murdered, he wanted to shut 'em up." Johnson had no clue of who killed Traiman or why, but he was now playing his hand.

"How you know if Black did it?" Johnson had her, Brown's question was that breaking point. Somerson nodded his head, amused at the just happenings.

"Now may we come in and talk?" Johnson asks, she was wounded prey and he was out for the kill. Brown stepped back and let them through.

"Brown, we know where Black's at. We need to know how to get to him." Johnson says, his voice still as smooth as water.

"You can't, you'll haft to wait him out.' Brown slowly says, her eyes getting glassy. Somerson was completely but silently shocked. He knew he could never make no one talk like this. Johnson you cold bastard. Somerson thought.

"Black's on a mission of some sort, something personal, I don't know what it is, but it's deeper than you think." Brown's words left Johnson wondering what she was talking about. Johnson decided not to pursue that information, because Brown wouldn't know Johnson had enough info, so he decided to leave Brown alone for the time being.

Johnson and Somerson, dismissed themselves from Brown's home, leaving her in tears, Johnson hoped she would do as he planned, lead them to Black himself. Brown thought about, how Rush told her it was Crusian, how easily he could lie. Brown wiped her eyes, she regained that ice, that momentarily vacated its place around her frigid heart.

Brown was now out, the game was over, she was used and dismissed. Brown looked around at her house, it was as barren as her life, empty and cold. Brown knew she had to changer her life, cancel that pain of loss.   Brown sat and stared into oblivion.

*   *   *   *

The Grand Doscine's lobby was packed full of guests scurrying about. On the elevator Black and Rush were on their way up to their floor. Through the glass encasing of the elevator, Black stared down, the people got smaller and smaller as they rose. Black and Rush rode up in a decimal silence, no words could match the volume of their thoughts.

The tremendous weight on Black's shoulders rivaled that of Atlas. His last confrontation with Crusian, left his mind in constant fluctuation. Black knew all of his people was straight, and that by now the feds done figured out his locale. He still

126

had the upper hand, they couldn't Rush in with guns, or risk trying to smoke Black out. Black smiled to himself.

They still can't get me, at least not yet, setting up shop here was good. Too many people, for them to get brash or bold. Crusian, what the fuck am I going to do about him. He's going to dime out, but he has to move fast, he knows shit is about to get ugly. Black's thoughts were halted as they got out on the Fifteenth floor.

Rush followed Black slowly into Black's room. The two took a seat, at the table over by the window. Black's room had view of the outside parking lot located in the back. There in that parking lot Black's gray Geo was parked. Black looked up at a thought entranced Rush.

"Everything's set?" Black asks, Rush took his time answering. He wanted to carefully word his response.

"Everything." Rush pauses for a moment. "San Fran my home dog, but his shit is hot though". Rush says, as if he was contemplating laying low once their ordeal was over. A silence fell again, Black pulled out one of his Queen cigars, bit off the end of it, and then lit it. He took a long pull, then slowly through his nostrils let the natural vapor go.

"Dog in this game, you gotta be slicker than grease on ice. Only a militant individual can make shit happen here. You got to learn how to cope. Who ever says this shit is easy money, is a dumb muthafucker with a degree bumming on some nickel, to dime shit. This is it baby; you either elevate the game, or be ass out in the long run". Black relays to a now surer Rush.

Black took another pull of his cigar. "So what's the deal with Brown?" Rush asks, Black shrugs his shoulders.

"Fuck that bitch, we have more pressing shit to attend to." Black says thinking about those twenty minutes of pleasure he frowned and decided to leave her alone.

"What's the deal with Reese?" Black asks, his voice tainted by the cigar's buzzing effect.

"He's doped up and laid out over in Mojo's room." Rush says, as he looked out the window, with his thoughts reflecting back to the night Dutch was supposed to lace Black's Geo. Slicker than Grease on ice, ain't that some shit. Rush thought. "Yo, my nigga I'm a go and check them niggas out. Get 'em ready for some real shit." Rush excuses himself from Black's room.

Black smiled to himself as his right-hand leaves. This nigga is colder than I thought, He's not even hot tempered no more. Damn I taught that nigga well. I just hope the nigga stays that way. But he'll learn when to amp himself, and blow those four fives when necessary. Black thought then pulled on his Queen once more, feeling the smoky relief in his lungs.

Once Rush was outside of Black's room, he was pulling out his cell phone as he glided down the hallway. Rush dialed a quick seven, Rush waited patiently while the phone on the other end rung. It rung twice before it was picked up.

"Crusian." A weary voice came across on the other line.

"Yea this Rush baby. Everything's set over here. What about yours?" Rush had no patience in his voice, Crusian took a deep breath, as he was coming down from a candy high.

"I'm on it, now, you must make sure Black is there and Ready.' Crusian was smiling as he spoke, he figured if he could convince Rush to take Black, he wouldn't have any blood on his hands.

"Crusian don't fuck with me. I'll have you spazing out like a fucking first timer.' Rush beeps out, not giving Crusian a chance to respond. Rush continued on down the hallway, with a twisted smile Rush was sizing up the money he would soon be counting.

Crusian was on a stellar high, as he was now dialing Somerson's number. Crusian waited patiently for the agent to pick up.

"Yea, Somerson here.' Somerson says, his mind still on getting at Black.

"Somerson, I have information that you would love." Crusian says, his high now halfway fallen from its peak. Somerson recognized the voice, he gave a tired sigh.

"What is it?" Somerson asks, being careful not to say Crusians name, as Johnson sat in the driver's seat.

"Black is moving out in a few days, so I suggest you make your arrest or killing very soon." So fuck the bullshit and get him out of the picture." Crusian then hangs up, leaving Somerson with a somewhat nervous feeling in his stomach. Crusian was finally feeling, that San Fran was finally his once more. On Somerson's end, him and Johnson were on their way back to San Fran.

Johnson was thinking about Brown's last words, from that last visit, she shed some light on why Black was in San Fran. Something personal, now what would Black have personal out here.

"Shay's Point!" Johnson's shouts aloud.

"What?" Somerson asks, surprised by Johnson sudden outburst.

"That's the reason why Black's out here. Berlin, Ron Plato, and now Crusian. They burnt down the place about a month ago. "Johnson conclusion made it a whole lot clearer of Black's being out in San Fran.

"I thought it was arson?" Somerson says, his concern ran parallel to his real knowledge of the situation.

"Man, the last time Black took something personal, he tied a witness up, and stripped her naked and burned her alive, in her bed. So when he takes something personal everyone involved in it, in street terms gets dun." Johnson's words caused Somerson to re-evaluate whom they were after.

If what Johnson says is true, then maybe he could catch Black after, Black does Crusian. Somerson smiled at those thoughts, get rid of two at one time. Things were looking good on both ends so far. Johnson was now marveled, he was wondering how he could've missed that. He knew Black wasn't dealing out here, it should've been obvious.

Johnson's thoughts paused, I thought it was arson? How the fuck, does he know what I'm talking about? Just like I thought, the fuckas in on it. Yea, I'm going to let him show his hand. Johnson looked over at Somerson then his eyes went back on the road. Later Johnson pulls to a stop in front of his hotel.

"I'll be back in the morning, to pick you up. I've got some planning to do, so be ready to move. I wanna do this shit fast." Somerson says, Johnson didn't respond to Somerson's statement. He just, in a nonchalant manner made his exit of the vehicle. Somerson slid over to the driver's side, and then pulled off slowly from the front of the hotel.

Johnson, was making his way to his room. He moved swiftly, glancing over his shoulder for his own safety. He didn't trust the atmosphere of San Fran, at that Westgates either. San Fran was too friendly on the stomach, and Johnson's gut was queezy from this case. Finally Johnson's room was in sight. He got their quick, his mind racing of possible ways of subduing Black.

Johnson pulled out his room key, the flat object shaped in a short rectangle, slid easily into the thin slot; Johnson pulled it out, and a green light flickered, as Johnson then made his way in. Johnson took a seat on the Queen size bed. Johnson relaxed, as his thoughts drifted back to that event with Veria.

The 31st Precinct was quiet that night, all's could be heard was Johnson's phone ringing, Johnson picked it up, he was still feeling good, on the fact that Shamon's case was just closed.

"Yea! Johnson speaking." Johnson says, his voice reflecting his joyous feelings.

"Johnson, this is Gordon, I have some bad news, Veria's been burned to death in her apartment".

"What happened?" Johnson screams into the receiver, shock now gripping his mind.

"It wasn't an accident, she was stripped naked, and tied to her bed. Johnson, I'm sorry." Gordon says, as he then hangs up. Johnson was seething with hatred, Black was the first person to come to his mind. Johnson cursed himself for not seeing that coming.

Johnson took a deep breath as he sprawled out across his plain sheet bed. A scary smile, crossed Johnson's grill, this opportunity Johnson, wouldn't be slighted on. This was his time to get revenge. Take Black back to Westgate and see him hang. Johnson was determined to make San Fran his last place of stands.

* * * *

The night was cool and distant, in it's strenuous darkness, stars fluttered above, playing a menacing game of dodge with looming clouds, that caused a slight fog. Rush was enjoying the jostling of both sides of the coin. He was in it for the money. Rush was creeping to the back parking lot. Rush paused for a moment, as he saw a man leaving the parking lot. The parking lot's dim lights obscured his vision.

From a brief moment of clarity, Rush identified the man as one of Crusian's men. Rush shook his head, he couldn't believe Crusian would double check his people's work. The cross has happened. Rush grabbed his heat, and retraced his steps back, to the hotel's entrance of the parking lot. As Rush walked down the brightly illuminated back halls of the Grand Doscines, he screwed on his silencer.

"Damn, these muthafuckas are here already. Black wouldn't change his plans without telling me right?" Shit, I told Crusian not to fuck with me, Yea now he's got to go. Fuck it I'll run San Fran by my mutherfucking self." Rush whispers to himself, as his frustration started to peak. Rush was hunting the man he'd spotted earlier.

Rush's brow was beaded up with sweat from tension. Rush was uneasy, he spots the man and then speeds up. The man didn't expect Rush to follow him, Rush put the gun up to the man's head. The man "froze". Rush thought about smoking the man, but decided instead to send Crusian a little message.

Rush drew back, and heavily slapped the man in the back of the head. The man fell instantly from the force of the blow. Rush repeatedly hit the man, in the face with the butt of his gun. Rush stopped short, only because he wanted the man to give Crusian a message.

"Muthafucka get up! Get up!" Rush yells at the semi-conscious man. The man could barely stand.

"Yea muthafucka, tell Crusian I'm through with this shit.' Rush says, then lets the man loose. Rush watched the man stagger back towards the back parking lot. Rush was starting to come into his own. The leadership of the dynasty was going to trade hands. Black ran it smoothly, as Rush would be the yang, to that remedy Black's yin was mixing.

Rush was in the same mind set, that Black had the night Veria burned to death. That calm infuriation of the mind, the cold inferno that seizes your soul, almost a coming of age experience. The drama moved Rush little, the malice Rush was feeling was enough for him to take, Crusian's last breath out of his chest.

As Rush moved through the Grand Doscines lobby. His cellular rang, Rush was caught off guard, he knew Crusians man wasn't that fast. Rush took the cell out of his pocket and beeped in.

"Yea." Rush's voice was icy hot.

"This me." Rush was surprised, he thought he would never hear or see Brown again.

"What's up?" Rush's question came across flat and cold, Brown lightly sighed on the other end.

"Johnson and Somerson came by. They know ya'll niggas are at the Grand Doscine. "Brown's answer came just as cold and flat.

"What else do they know?" Rush's mind was further ahead of any response. Brown could come up with. He knew she broke down, he heard those sour notes in her voice.

"Nothing, but they coming cousin, and I hope they fucking get all ya'll; punk muthafuckers!" Brown's tone brought on a cold grin on Rush's face. She must've found out Black had Traimen killed. Rush thought. Rush hung up on Brown, to him the conversation, took an irrelevant turn. Rush was now in a calm hurry. He had to let Black in on the just happenings.

Rush smiled to himself, what am I worrying about, Black probably already knew. That niggas been illing lately. He knows, I hope this shit he wants done works.

* * * *

The morning rolled in with a smiling sunrise, Somerson was outside waiting on Johnson. Somerson was planning all night with Roberson, saving his career seamed to give Somerson tireless energy. All was left was to get Johnson up to date on the plan. Johnson finally walked out the front entrance of the hotel. Somerson watched as Johnson shielded his eyes from the beaming sun.

Once inside the car, Johnson remained silent. Somerson noticing Johnson's odd facial expression, caught the hint of Johnson's feelings from his quietness. Somerson skipped the usual formalities and got straight to the point.

"Here's the plan, its the usual sit and wait. Tap the phone lines, 24-7 surveillance." Somerson quickly says. "It's just normal procedure." Johnson shock his head. He knew that simple shit wouldn't catch Black. The one thing that played on Johnson's mind was, why would Black paint himself into a corner like this. He was smarter than that.

Johnson felt like, they were being herded towards this hotel, for some sort of slaughter. Johnson, was for the first time in this lustrous career, stomped, it all didn't add up. Somerson glanced at the unusually quiet Johnson. Johnson to Somerson seamed absent for the moment. As they came to a stop on 19th Street. Johnson was still lost in thought.

"Somerson, tapping the phone lines is useless, they communicate through cells. They even speak in code. You can watch all day and never once see Black." Johnson pauses. "Their planning something, its just that I don't know what." In Johnson's voice, you could hear the tiredness that sounded off like gunshots through his words.

"So what you think we should do, go in guns blazing" Somerson laughed at his own words. Johnson smiled.

"That's a damn good idea. "Johnson looked around, the passing streets. "Somerson, where the hell are we going?" Johnson asked, curious, as everything looked unfamiliar.

"We're going to Roberson's house. He's got the final deal on the plans." Somerson answers. His enthusiasm helped a little to liven up Johnson's somber mood.

"Crusian's place was full of tension, as the man Rush has just recently beat to a pulp, told Crusian of Rush's message. Crusian sat back in his recliner chair, peeved at being played. Crusian had Rush pegged as an easy mark. He didn't realize he was the one marked. Crusian now knew Black was a wild card.

Crusian had to get rid of Black, but the blood that would be on his hands, would drag Omant into the picture. Which meant his death if that happened. Crusian had to think fast, time was a vital part of the equasion and Crusian was running out of it. Crusian picked up his cordless phone and then dialed Somerson's number.

"Yea, Somerson." Somerson says, still ampted by his plans to catch Black.

"Yea, this Crusian we've got to talk." Crusian's voice sounded urgent. Somerson's mood was now shot.

"Yea, I'm working on that now as we speak." Somerson spoke quick, trying to get the conversation over with. Crusians patience was now little if any at all. Crusian hung up the phone. Crusian called Juan into the room, Crusian's panic was hidden in a deep scowl which was now placed upon an nervous Juan.

"Get Dutch and the rest of the boys ready. We're moving on Black tonight". Juan was instantly on the move, to carry out Crusian's orders. Crusian set back, still amazed at how he allowed himself to be played into such a baitful plot. The phone started ringing, Crusian looked at the phone not wanting to answer it.

"Yes, this is Crusian."

"Crusian its me Somerson". Crusian's face went to semi-smile, Somerson has never called him before.

"Good news?" Crusian asks, his voice for the first time showing no anger. Somerson found a way, to get away from Johnson and Roberson, by retreating to the upstairs bathroom.

"Here's the deal where watching the Grand Doscine, be there and watch the fireworks tonight". Crusian smiled at Somerson's words. He gets to watch Black finally fold up.

"That was already in the making Somerson" But Somerson if your people don't get Black, mine will, you do understand?" Crusian says venomously.

"I understand". Somerson says, before he beeps out. Crusian was now all smiles; he was going to get Somerson and Black both.

The afternoon hours flowed rather smoothly, as Black and his people prepared, for their final night's stay at the lush Grand Doscine.

"Is Reese ready yet? This shit has to be perfect. We don't have much time left." Black asks Rush, whom seemed rather quiet for these last intense moments.

"Yea he's ready, and so is Mojo, Charlie Ave and his crew is also ready." Rush says, with his mind still preoccupied by his situation with Crusian.

"The fuck nigga!" Black yells, noticing Rush's lapse of concentration.

"I need your full attention here, you can think about presidents later." Rush cut Black a curious look, he thought Black was bugging out for a minute; but Rush knew better than that. Black was directing Rush's attention, Black knew if Rush wasn't fully mentally set, this wouldn't churn right. Rush walked out the room slowly, his mind still a little affected by the dueling situations.

Black knew he had done enough to get rush's mind on track. Black at this point, was as calm as a breezeless summer night. Black poured a glass of Dark, on ice, with some lemon wedges mixed. Black caught a hot but relaxing feeling as he took a long sip. As Black's lungs burned, so did his heated, diligent thoughts.

This is it my nigga; the ninth inning, you've played hard and moved swiftly. You've taken over New York finally, and you're still with a wicked ass team. Tonight's the night baby. Lead those stupid mutherfuckers to the slaughter. Ya, they know where I'm at, come and get me mutherfuckas. Anthony Blackmon, you've outdone yourself baby.

A rare smile crossed Black's face, as he took another long sip of his Darkly colored elixir. In the next room, a sleeping Reese was being woke up by an irritated Rush.

"Yo, nigga get up and put these clothes on." Rush yells at a semi-conscious Reese. Reese was severely groggy, as he reached for the clothes that Rush had thrown on the queen size bed. Mojo sat at a table that was cluttered with shot glasses, as he was downing straight whiskey, to keep his blood flow in irrigation.

Rush was now facing the rooms window. A weird frown, seemingly teasing, gave rush's face an endless tired expression. Tired as in viscously intended. Rush checked his pager for time, it was running out, running away fast. Rush glanced back over his shoulder at a now fully dressed Reese.

"Mojo, give this nigga something to sober his ass up, and stop drinking that shit, we need you sober too, for tonight". Rush's words were immediately met, as Mojo put down his shot glass of whiskey, and went to get some coffee for Reese. Rush knew shit had to be straight, even though Mojo might be some what blitzed, that's when he was at his most dangerous. Rush knew Mojo would pull through for the night.

"Black found himself alone, for the first time in a good minute. He could feel, the hot breath of the law lingering on his neck. As the smoke drifted from Black's cigar, Black analyzed his thoughts, he was thrilled, the end game, the mystique of the outcome, it was Black's addiction he loved the game, a generous living for the winner; a ridiculous embarrassment for the looser.

The flow of the drama, had Black's mind in a calm ingenious state. He couldn't wait for the night to start, only three more hours to six. Black pulled out his chrome, and stared at it with a radiant gleam in his eyes. Black took a long pull off his cigar. As the vapors drifted out of his nose, Black felt more relaxed; he's reached the pinnacle of this game.

Johnson and Somerson, were setting their plans in motion, agents flooded the vacinity of the outskirts of the Grand Doscine. Johnson was feeling ancy, he didn't know what to expect. Somerson's ancyness was stimulating from the idea of saving his rope-a-dope career. Somerson knows where Crusian would be, so it was set, now all was left was to trap Black.

As the evening hours creeped in so did plain clothes agents. They took up discreet positions around the lobby. They were so smooth, and blended so well, chameleons couldn't hide from them. They kept a watchful eye for Black. Outside the hotel Johnson and Somerson sat waiting. Johnson thought back to all of his plans that failed to catch Black.

The one that stood out the most, the one that never took root. Toi Sanchez, it was perfect, but it was just Johnson's luck when Shay's Point burned down. He was finally going to get his closure, but this felt like a real good set-up. Dealing with Black, caused Johnson to learn, that Black's always a step ahead of his opposition.

"This isn't right Somerson, my guts telling me. This shit isn't what it seems." Johnson's voice held sincere notes of doubt.

"Come on Johnson; maybe your boy Black isn't as smart as you thought, because if he was, why would he let us get this close." Somerson's optimistic, point of view, eased Johnson's mind very little.

"You don't know him like I do, he's a sick bastard, but not stupid." Somerson says through his smile. "Dead or alive we're getting our man tonight." Johnson wished he could take Somerson's confidence in a good manner, but he couldn't ignore his gut, something was wrong and he knew it. Somerson was too assuring, Johnson figured that Somerson had the inside track, he was in on something, or in with someone involved on the crooked end. Johnson made that mistake with his partner Tolip back in Westgate, and wasn't going that route again.

Johnson tried to relax, but his stomach was bubbling due to anticipation, he felt like he was back on the beat in Philly. Too eager for the action, Johnson knew those type of feelings could get you killed in the field. So Johnson checked himself, before he would fall victim to over anticipating. Somerson sat in silence his eyes reflecting the orange rays of the starting sunset.

Somerson's thoughts were coming heated, broken like, in cascades of tempered fevers. Chills violated his spine, he awaited this final moment, in a few hours his career would flourish. The man who brought down Crusian Ramone, and whom helped hunt down Anthony Blackmon. These thoughts brought on a hidden smile in Somerson's diluted mind.

Back inside the hotel Charlie Ave, Surpreme, and Majestic, were draped in black apparel. On the bed sat three oozies, two nines, and a Saturday night special. Charlie Ave began to place silencers on the weapons. Their part of the plan; was to alleviate the extra pressure concerning the parties involved. Majestic pulled another duffel bag out from the queen size bed.

Majestic pulled out the clips for the oozies and nines, and hollow points for the revolver. Supreme sat back, monitoring the door. They didn't want any unwanted visitors. In the silent atmosphere of the room, guns being cocked and loaded was the sweet music filling that void in the room.

"Supreme, pass that blunt nigga!" Charlie raves, as he couldn't resist, the luring call of the thick smoke. Majestic smiled as he loaded the oozies. He didn't need a stimulant, to activate his ravaging mind. The oozies were set, silencers, full clips, and itchy trigger fingers ready to pull the crescent moon shaped triggers. Charlie put the blunt out, looked at Supreme and Majestic.

"Ya'll niggas ready to move. It's going to be some shit tonight". Charlie Ave says, as this was his way of giving a rather twisted pep talk. In a brief movement, Charlie and his people made their way out of the room. With their weapons concealed, they silently made their way down the dimly lit hallway of the Grand Doscine. As they made their way by Black's room, Charlie knocked twice, letting Black know that they were on their way.

Black smiled t himself when he heard the signaling knock on the door. Black put down his cigar, grabbed his chrome and cane, and began to go over to Mojo's room. Black with an infuriated ease made his way down the hall. Once in front of Mojo's room door, Black gripped his chrome tighter. With his cane Black knocked twice. The door slowly opened. Rush greeted Black with a cold look.

"That nigga ready?" Black's question was answered by a cold nodding Rush. Black eased by Rush, and on into the room. Reese was sitting on the bed, with a scowl on his face; Reese's attention focussed on Black.

"What the fuck nigga, why you got me here like this?" Mojo pulled his hammer back of his revolver. Mojo had it drawn on

Reese while they waited on Black. The sound of the hammer begin pulled, caught Reese's undivided attention.

"You're here to do one final thing for me Reese. Ain't this some shit, I knew about how you were snitching to Johnson about my shit. This is pay back muthafucker'. Black drew back his cane and with the butt of it, slapped Reese in the mouth with it. chipped and full teeth flew everywhere, as Reese spun helplessly to the floor.

Mojo picked up, the now bloody, yucky-mouthed Reese. Resse held his mouth in obvious pain. Rush smiled knowing Black was thought this plan well through.

"Clean this nigga up we've only got one hour. "Black tells Mojo coldly, whom was laughing in sheer amusement.

Crusian, Juan and Dutch, loaded up the Bently. The three were on their way to the Grand Doscine. This was going to be Crusian's night, all of his problems solved, with one swift great blow. All Crusian needed to see, was Black being apprehended, then he himself would deal with Somerson. As the Bently gave a luxurious ride, Crusians mind was like live shock wires.

Crusian's thoughts were heavy, not of despair, but of uncertain ancyness. Crusian knew if they didn't get Black tonight San Fran would be a war zone by morning.

Crusian's schedule was tight, he was to receive a shipment from Omant in the morning, so Crusian was playing the odds for the night's hopeful success.

Passing nineteenth Street, meant only a ten more minute drive. Crusian sat in the back seat, soaking wet, drowning in the deep depths of his own pressure filled thoughts. Crusian wanted back his control. He would've never guessed, that someone like Black, would've caused him so much strife. Crusian while thinking stroked his chin, he was unaware, of the events that would unfold in the night that hauntingly awaited him.

The Bently moved with the same descending speed of the setting sun. Crusian knew in his heart, that this night would tell all. He knew the list, Berlin, Ron, and next up Crusian, himself.

"Juan, were going to park on the hill, we're going to get a good look at what is to happen." Crusian tells a relaxed Juan. Crusian projected his focus over to Dutch.

"Did you do what I asked?" Crusian's question, brought a wicked smile to Dutch's face.

"Yes, its going to be very bright". Dutch answers, his colorful metaphors, brought on an unlikely smile to Crusian's uneasy face.

The Bently cruised with an orderly energy. Crusian and his people's mind were set. The sky was a stormy array of fiery colors. Crusian couldn't' relax, the intensity of the situation, left him hard pressed for soothing emotions. The Grand Doscine, the name hung in Crusian's mind like bait on a hook. Crusian hated to admit, but Black's game play was exquisitely crafted.

Dutch pulled out his nine and check it, it was for that extra precaution. Juan pulled to a slow stop. The Grand Doscine was in sight. The hill they were on helped them see the back parking lot. The Grand Doscine stood towering over them, as they parked the Bently on the red sanded lot. Now all was left was to wait the situation out.

"What time is it?" Black asks, a slow pacing Rush looked at his platinum Mavado.

"Twenty minutes to six. It's starting to get dark, yo." Rush says, his pause gave away his question, Black got his response ready.

"How you going to move with this?" Rush's question is just what Black expected. Rush was ready, Black smiled to himself.

"through the back, ten minutes . . . Rush don't be late. I need you, to walk me to my car". Rush nodded in an understanding way. Rush was now on his way to Mojo's room. The hallway seemed longer than usual. Rush's thoughts were dropping like heavy baselines. Mojo's door finally appears, Rush knocked twice but not too hard.

The door slowly opened, Mojo was set, with his coat on and pistol in hand. He smiled at an nonchalant Rush.

"Yo, when you get that nigga to the spot, call me. I should be set up by then. Just before you call me get in contact with Korlane First. I'll tell you the rest later. One baby." Rush says then gives Mojo some dap and slides easily back down the hallway. Mojo goes back into his room, and gets a good seat by his window.

Meanwhile, outside the Grand Doscine, watching were Somerson and Johnson.

"Damn, it's getting dark quick. This is when Black really plays." Johnson says, his voice a ghostly whisper, that seemed to float on Somerson's seemingly deaf ears. Somerson ignored his whinny partner. His partner, an uncomfortable Johnson, still held onto his gut feeling.

Johnson felt the situation for what it really was. Johnson knew this was a set up. This proved his suspicions of Somerson being crooked. From years of experience, Johnson knew a personal agenda when he saw one. Johnson himself had as just an agenda. Loosing a partner by the slaying of a gun, is a certified reason for wanting this person. But the way Somerson acts, it seemed as though, the man's life was on the line.

Somerson's personal agenda, clouded all reasoning and judgment, and somewhat obscured a once rather good agent. Johnson's eyes never left the immense sight of the Grand Doscine.

[6 PM The Vacinity of the Grand Doscine]

The sky was a menacing, ebony related color. Stars shimmered in their heated glory. As on the ground, the back parking lot was under heavy surveillance. The feds had people everywhere. The door leading from the Grand Doscine was starting to open. Two men emerged, both draped in jet black apparel. Somerson and Johnson kept a watchful eye on the two men.

Johnson identified Rush but couldn't get a look at the man next to him. He couldn't see if it was Black or not.

142

"Let them get into the car, then turn the dogs loose." Johnson's words, were the same as Somerson's thoughts. the two watched the scene intently. Somerson radioed his people to wait on his word. Inside the Grand Doscine, looking out of his window, stood a perplexed Mojo. This was his cue to move out the remaining party.

Mojo made one motion towards the door, Mojo was now making his way to the parking garages. Mojo glanced around, he had a cocked eye for the fives and agents. Mojo pulled the keys out to his rent-a-car. Being on the third level of the garage, Mojo's cue to leave would be very viewable. Mojo made it to his car, once inside he pulled a blunt out and lit it.

Mojo knew, he only had a few minutes, to get out once the signal was given. So he sat patiently and waited. But on the hill, Mojo's brethren, Charlie Ave, Surpreme, and Majestic. Were on the move, with their oozies in hand, Charlie Ave, and his people got out of their car. they moved in the silence of the night.

Crusian, and his people weren't expecting this type of move. Blind to his surroundings, Crusian was preoccupied by the back parking lot's scenery. Charlie and his crew was moving right on time. Charlie cocked his oozie, this should be easy and quiet. Then it happened.

Boom!!! Boom!!!

The explosion shook the ground, as a huge orange cloud erupted, from the Grand Doscines back parking lot. On this note Charlie Ave and his people let loose on Crusians car. they fired till their clips were fully emptied into the cars inner interior. The force of the hollow points, left the doors full of huge holes. To make sure the job was done thoroughly.

Charlie brought out his thirty-eight, and walked up closer to the Bently. Once up on it, Charlie saw the wasted mass of Crusian and his people. Charlie smiled to himself, he turned to his crew and smiled. Surpreme and Majestic knew that their part of the plan was finished. They wondered how everything else was going.

The police and Feds, were all over the back parking lot within minutes, of the explosion. They apprehended Rush, but Rush showed no worries, as they had nothing on him, being guilty of association, carried no time. He would be out in hours. Johnson and Somerson knew it was now over. With Black dead so was the dynasty, all was left to wrap the case up.

"Damn, I wanted him alive, but I was cheated by his own death. I can't win for loosing." Johnson says shaking his head. This was Johnson's closure, finally his partner could rest in peace.

"Yea, but as they say, what you put out in this world, comes back to you ten times worse. And this fuck got what he deserved." Somerson says, in response to Johnson's comment earlier. On in the inside Somerson was now fully relieved of all pressure. Imagine the glee, he would feel, when he finds out, Crusian was dead also. The two left the crime scene their hearts still feeling the anguish and lonely pain.

Johnson and Somerson shook hands and congratulated each other on a job well done.

*   *   *   *

Now switching from 210 to Interstate 5, was a quick moving Mojo, his destination Tijuana. Mojo was carrying some real important merchandise. Once there Mojo thought about retiring. That to him seemed to cap a most perfect year.

*   *   *   *

Epilogue

[One Week Later]

The sun was blazing, as San Fran was still a buzz. The events of a week ago, set Rush's mind in motion, Rush was relaxed, his current situation, had his life looking plush. The yang to Black's smooth and strong yin. Rush was enjoying being the front man, of the dynasty. The feds kept an open eye for Rush.

Rush was wise to this plight, he let Mojo run the field. While he played the low. Out in New York, Korlane and BaiRute, made a formidable team to deal with. They recently established the dynasties presence on the Islands of Hellgate. Leroy and Brandy opened Black's club: The Blaq Abstract, basically a duplicate in design of Shay's Point. The Dynasty was strong as ever.

Rush's relaxation was disturbed by the high pitched ringing of the phone. Rush picked the phone up slowly.

"State your business." Rush's voice echoed with the relaxing heat, that was soothing his mind.

"What's the deal baby?" The voice on the other end brought a wide grin to Rush's face.

"Black! What's the word my nigga. You chilling and shit?" Rush says excitedly. Black paused catching himself before he revealed his location. "Yo I heard, Reese went up in a blaze." Black finishes.

"Yo, that shit was pretty, shit was this huge orange cloud. Shit was just pretty." Rush says knowing, Black could picture what he was saying. Black was in the trunk of Mojo's car when the explosion happened.

"Damn, remember slicker than Grease on Ice, its the only way to survive this game." Black's voice was freezing serious.

"No doubt." Rush responds, almost humble in tone.

"Ten seconds, one, I'm out." Black beeped out. Rush smiled. Ten seconds more, the Feds would have 'em traced. Rush was feeling hellishly blessed. The sun was still blazing, but it was cold inside of Rush's mind. Black left a legacy. It was now Rush's order to control. Rush walked over to the sliding door to his patio.

Rush slowly slid the glass door back, he stepped onto the patio. With one breath he inhaled the San Fran's fresh crooked air. Rush was finally home. For the first time ever, the world was his, the soul controller.

*　*　*　*

Johnson was back in Westgate enjoying the feel of the cool weather, compared to the heat in San Fran, it was a welcoming feeling. Finally this man got a piece of mind.

Johnson's closure was complete, Tolip could rest, but Johnson still had the feeling something wasn't right. Johnson's let the feeling go, as he let the hot whiskey flow.

Damn it's finally over. Johnson thought with a smile.

www.ingramcontent.com/pod-product-compliance
Lightning Source LLC
Chambersburg PA
CBHW020438290526
45785CB00002B/909